HOW TO PUBLISH A CHURCH NEWSLETTER

Revised Edition

GEORGE W. KNIGHT

Broadman Press
Nashville, Tennessee

4231-17

ISBN: 0-8054-3117-9

Dewey Decimal Classification: 254.4

Subject Headings: PUBLIC RELATIONS—CHURCHES // NEWSPAPERS, RELIGIOUS

Library of Congress Catalog Card Number: 88-22973

Printed in the United States of America

Library of Congress Cataloging-in-Publication Data

Knight, George W. (George Wendell), 1940-
    How to publish a church newsletter / George W. Knight.—Rev. ed.
        p.   cm.
    Includes bibliographical references and index.
    ISBN 0-8054-3117-9 (pbk.)
    1. Church newsletters—Publishing.   I. Title.
Z286.R4K59 1989
686.2'2—dc19   88-22973

Contents

Introduction: Catching a Vision

The parish newsletter is one of the most effective promotional tools in the church today. Congregations use the newsletter to keep members informed about important events, to enrich their faith, and to cultivate the fellowship of the entire company of faith. The church paper is quick, convenient, and inexpensive—an ideal way to communicate regularly with every member of the church.

Newsletters are now so widely used by churches of all denominations and sizes that it's hard to imagine a time when they didn't exist. But a quick glance at the volume numbers of a sampling of newsletters reveals that few have been around for longer than fifty years. There was little need for newsletters during the first half of this century. Churches were small, and the programs they offered were basic and simple.

But all that changed with the "religious boom" of the 1950s. Suburban churches mushroomed. Older, established churches increased dramatically in membership. Keeping up with members and getting them involved became more of a problem. The programs offered by churches became more complicated, as music activities, youth programs, church library services, and recreational-family life activities became more popular. These have expanded in recent years to include special activities for senior adults and single adults and attention to such social issues as world hunger and world peace. This proliferation of programs and concerns will probably continue in the years ahead as our society becomes more complex.

The logical answer to these diverse promotional needs of the modern church is the newsletter, mailed regularly to members as well as prospects. No other medium of communication is better suited for the task of keeping the church informed about all these important concerns.

But the sad thing is that too many churches have failed to catch a vision of what their newsletters can accomplish among the membership. This brings us around to the purpose of this book. It should reveal some possibilities for your newsletter that you've never considered before. It's designed to *show* you how to publish a newsletter that is positive, dynamic, challenging, and motivating to your readers—one that's strictly first class in every way.

Notice the emphasis on the word *show*. This book is illustrated with scores of clippings from church newsletters. These are both good and bad examples of how to put a church paper together. These authentic case studies should make the book much more useful as a production guide. My thanks to the churches of all denominations who provided newsletters for this type of analysis.

My thanks also to Lucy Hoskins, church administration consultant at the Sunday School Board, Nashville, Tennessee, for her gentle but firm insistence that I should write this book. Her advice and counsel have made the book an especially useful tool for church secretaries, those competent servants of the church who usually get stuck with the task of "putting out the newsletter." We hope this book will simplify their job and give them a feeling of confidence in this important responsibility.

GEORGE W. KNIGHT

Preface to the Revised Edition

Since the publication of the first edition of this book in 1983, thousands of churches have applied its suggestions to help refine and improve their newsletters. Others have used the book as an orientation manual for new secretaries to help them understand the detailed process of newsletter production.

This revised edition of *How to Publish a Church Newsletter* should make it even more useful for both these purposes. An entire chapter on the use of the computer in newsletter production has been added. Since computers are becoming more and more common around church offices, all newsletter editors should be aware of the possibilities of the new technology known as "desktop publishing."

Other helpful features of this revised edition include more information on copying machines and mailing systems, an expanded chapter on specialized resources for better newsletter production, and an index to the book's contents to help you find information on a specific subject quickly and easily.

My thanks to John Chandler and Brooks Faulkner of the Church Administration Department of the Sunday School Board, Nashville, Tennessee, for their encouragement in this revision project. We hope the book will continue to serve as an authoritative guide for church newsletter editors for many years to come.

GEORGE W. KNIGHT

1
An Approach to Your Job
As Newsletter Editor

Let's call her "Conscientious Connie." She's an efficient secretary who, among other assorted duties, is responsible for writing, typing, printing, and mailing the church newsletter, *The Calvary Clarion*. Connie likes her job. She thinks of it as a real place of service. But sometimes the hassle of publishing the newsletter issue after issue tends to get her down.

Take last week, for example. First, Mrs. Floogle called, two days past the deadline, to insist on a notice in *The Clarion* about the quarterly planning meeting of her Sunday School class. Connie worked hard to squeeze the article in, although it meant shortening some other items that she had already typed. Then she made phone calls to six different committee members to gather some important facts. These had not been included in an article on next week's big stewardship event. Naturally, the person who was responsible for convening this committee had left town on a business trip shortly after turning in the article.

Finally, Connie got the entire issue typed and arranged neatly into pages. Then the minister had second thoughts and made several changes in his "Pastor to People" column. Back to the typewriter Connie went, mumbling something about "church people" and how she was beginning to feel "called" to a "secular job."

Sound familiar? There's probably something of Connie in every person who has served as editor of the newsletter on a church staff. Let's be honest and admit from the very beginning that putting out a church paper issue after issue is no picnic. Even on the best days, it's a task that would tax the patience of Job. Versatility and flexibility are essential. You have to jump through more hoops than the acrobats at the circus to get all the information together before the next deadline.

Rewards of the Job

But this is not the only side of the job. For every hassle there is an equal and compensating reward. Perhaps the greatest is the feeling that you are involved in something that is really positive and worthwhile. Think about the scores of newspapers and magazines in the marketplace that are filled with pessimism and bad news. They focus on the negative side of human existence—crime, unemployment, the faltering economy, war, human degradation, and suffering.

Church newsletters are cut from a different piece of cloth. Because they represent the hope which the church finds in Jesus Christ, they are channels of joy, thanksgiving, and love. This doesn't mean that churches and their newsletters should deny the existence of evil and suffering. It simply says that our calling is to sound the note of hope and victory that a broken world needs to hear in the midst of its pain. Isn't it nice to be involved in a publication that is so positive and optimistic in its approach to life? That has to rate as one of the top satisfactions of editing and producing your church newsletter.

Another real plus of newsletter work is the potential it offers for creative expression. Some jobs around the church office—typing, filing, financial posting, for example—may become routine after you have performed them for a while. But putting together the church paper doesn't have to become boring and dull.

To keep this from happening, fight the tendency to take the path of least resistance in producing your newsletter. Put some serious thought and planning into each individual issue. Don't do the same thing over and over again. Arrange your copy, headlines, and illustrations together in such a way that the paper comes across as fresh, new, and exciting every time your readers pick it up. This is not easy to do, of course, but whoever said that creative work is a snap?

Take a good look at the two church newsletters reproduced on page 11. See the difference between the *routine* approach and the *creative* approach? One of these editors obviously invests a lot more effort to make her publication interesting and readable. Each issue of the newsletter offers you the chance to be just as forceful and dynamic. So take a deep breath, flex your mental muscles, and thank God for the opportunity to be creative in your work.

Needed: A Systems Approach

A healthy attitude toward your task as newsletter editor will get you started. But only the right organization and the proper tools will keep you working efficiently at the job day after day. Two things that make any kind of publishing work unique are unbending time pressures (deadlines) and the need for attention to details. You can master your job as church newsletter editor by establishing control over these two important phases of the task. To do this, use a systems approach—set up definite plans and procedures for getting the job done.

Deadlines and Schedules

Even mature adults have been known to cringe at the word *deadline*. It comes across as harsh and restrictive. But few worthwhile things have been accomplished without deadlines. They are necessary and specific time schedules against which church newsletter editors must work to make sure the church paper gets out on time.

Deadlines for each issue. The more often you publish your church newsletter, the tighter your deadlines have to be. If you issue weekly, for example, you can't afford to miss the outgoing mail by even a few hours. This might cause the newsletter to arrive a day or two late, canceling out much of the promotional value of that particular issue. Deadlines for getting all copy submitted to the editor must be set early enough to allow plenty of production time for each weekly issue.

Most churches that publish weekly have the paper in the mail on Wednesday afternoon or Thursday morning. This is essential so it can be delivered by the post office on Thursday and Friday—certainly no later than Saturday. One successful secretary-editor observes the following schedule of deadlines to make sure the paper is always ready for the Thursday morning mail.

WEEKLY NEWSLETTER PRODUCTION SCHEDULE

- **Thursday:** Meet with the church staff to plan newsletter for the next week.

- **Friday:** Compile materials; write articles and announcements.

- **Monday:** Write other articles, based on events and announcements growing out of the services over the weekend.

- **Tuesday:** Do camera-ready paste-up of all pages for the newsletter. Have paste-ups ready for pickup that afternoon by local contract printer.

- **Wednesday:** Newsletter printed by printer and delivered to church by late afternoon.

- **Thursday:** Label, sort, and package all newsletters for mailing and deliver to local post office. Thursday afternoon, meet with church staff to plan newsletter for the next week.

Notice that this editor's production schedule follows a cycle of exactly seven days. She does the same jobs at the same time week after week. This establishes a routine that helps the work go rapidly and efficiently.

If your church publishes twice a month or monthly, your deadlines won't be as crucial. But you still need a definite schedule like the one shown to keep the work moving. Start with the date when the paper needs to be in the mail. Then back up from that date to allow yourself the time you need to get each issue compiled, edited, designed, printed, and prepared for mailing.

Once you've established a schedule of deadlines, make sure every member of the church staff knows about it. Make a list for the minister and post it in his office, particularly if he has a habit of procrastinating and running late with his column. Better still, publish the deadlines in the newsletter regularly to let all church members know about the ground rules.

Even after publishing the newsletter deadlines, you'll probably still receive some late articles. But at least you'll have something in print you can show the offending church members to prove you aren't just trying to be difficult. The reproduction from one church newsletter on page 12 shows what might be included in your policy statement about deadlines and other important procedures. Publish it several times during the year to give it good exposure.

A long-range planning schedule. Precise scheduling from issue to issue is one ingredient of success in newsletter publishing. But the editors who really do a first-class job are those who have learned the secret of long-range planning. There's no reason why you can't project and assign some features in your newsletter ahead of time, perhaps weeks or even months before they are due. By working ahead like this, you are more likely to enlist talented church members who will agree to take on special writing assignments for the newsletter.

Begin your long-range planning by thinking about these four types of material that are covered in most church papers: (1) events of the Christian year, (2) holidays on the secular calendar, (3) concerns that are unique to your denomination, and (4) special programs, events, and traditions of your own church.

The nice thing about all four of these categories is that most of the dates are already set well in advance. Events of the Christian year, holidays on the secular calendar, and denominational concerns are always precisely dated and known ahead of time. And your church probably has a good idea at the beginning of the year about the dates for its own special events, such as revivals, retreats, anniversary celebrations, and stewardship promotion.

To do long-range projection of content for your newsletter, write all these events down in calendar fashion, listing them by months from January through December or throughout the church year. Make special notes about newsletter features and articles that can be assigned *now* to support some of these special events. Your completed planning sheet might look something like this:

Long-Range Plans
Special Features for *The Calvary Clarion*
January-December

January

Emphases: New Year's Day, Layman's Sunday, Epiphany Sunday, Make-Your-Will Stewardship Focus

Supporting Newsletter Features: (1) Special column by associate pastor on "Getting the Jump on Your New Year's Resolutions"; (2) 200-word article by Earl Hawkins, attorney, on "The Stewardship Dimension of a Christian's Will"

February

Emphases: World Brotherhood Sunday, Valentine's Day, Lincoln's Birthday, Washington's Birthday

Supporting Newsletter Feature: Valentine's feature, with photos, on Ralph and Lillian Crawford, church's oldest couple, celebrating their 58th anniversary this year

March

Emphases: Youth Week, St. Patrick's Day

Supporting Newsletter Features: (1) Articles, with photos, on church youth who will be leading in Youth Week services; (2) brief, printed testimonies from Pam Smallwood and Mike Martin on "Bearing My Witness as a Christian Teenager"

April

Emphases: Holy Week, Passion Sunday, Good Friday, Easter, Lent

Supporting Newsletter Features: (1) Special column by the senior minister on "How to Get Ready for the Lenten Season"; (2) extended feature, with photos, on special music for the church's observance of Holy Week

May

Emphases: Mother's Day, Memorial Day, Pentecost Sunday, Christian Family Week, graduation

Supporting Newsletter Features: (1) Excerpt of Memorial Day sermon, "Lest We Forget," by the senior minister; (2) publication of children's Mother's Day notes to their mothers, an educational activity in the first-grade department of Sunday School

June

Emphases: Vacation Church School, Father's Day, Trinity Sunday, annual church picnic

Supporting Newsletter Features: (1) Special picture page, candid shots of members having fun at annual picnic in Lafayette Park; (2) article recognizing and thanking workers who helped in the annual Vacation Church School

July

Emphases: Independence Day, summer missions project

Supporting Newsletter Feature: Special article, with photos, on church youth going to inner-city congregation in Kingston to conduct mission Vacation Church Schools

August

Emphases: World Hunger Sunday, church's observance of 15th anniversary

Supporting Newsletter Features: (1) Column by minister of education on "What Can One Christian Do About World Hunger?" (2) 200-word article by Dr. Redford, charter member, on the early days of our church's history

September

Emphases: Labor Day, Grandparents Day

Supporting Newsletter Feature: Focus on senior adults of the church and retired members who give many hours of service to special church projects

October

Emphases: Reformation Sunday, Halloween, annual stewardship emphasis and adoption of church budget

Supporting Newsletter Features: (1) Publication of new church budget with explanation of various ministries which church supports; (2) printed stewardship testimonies of 15 words each by Brian Hollaway, Mildred Nelson, and Troy Mickelson

November

Emphases: Election Day, Veteran's Day, Thanksgiving

Supporting Newsletter Feature: Brief printed letters from 8-10 members on "The Things About My Church for Which I'm Thankful"

December

Emphases: Advent, Christmas, the music of Christmas

Supporting Newsletter Features: (1) Article by the minister of music about the two or three all-time favorite Christmas carols of the church and how they came to be written; (2) photo feature on the Singing Christmas Tree, an annual presentation of the music ministry of the church

After you've finished your planning, follow up immediately to enlist the people who have been targeted as writers for these special features. If some won't accept assignments, contact others who can do the job. Working ahead like this gives you time to make alternate plans if your first approach doesn't work out.

For better long-range planning, get other members of the church staff involved in sharing their dreams and ideas for the newsletter. If you're lucky enough to have a staff of writers and reporters, they should also be included in this planning process. They are more likely to follow through on their assignments if they have a say in the overall plans.

Dealing with Details

While long-range planning is essential, you can't afford to be so concerned about tomorrow that you forget about the day-to-day details of the job. The little details can make your life miserable unless you take them just as seriously as the big things. Accept that as a fact of life. It goes along with the job.

Double-check names and facts. One of the things you should learn to do automatically is to check all names and facts for accuracy before publishing them in the newsletter. Even church people can be unforgiving if you misspell their names. And if Mr. and Mrs. John Jones are the proud parents of a six-pound daughter, they certainly don't want it reported in the newsletter as a seven-pound, eight-ounce son! Learn to check all names and facts to make sure you have them right.

News items that are called in by telephone are a particular problem. Ask church members to spell out all names and facts that leave any room for confusion or misinterpretation. The proper name Catherine, for example, can also be spelled Kathryn or Katherine. The one way you'll know for sure is to ask the caller to spell it out. Do this routinely with all information that is called in by telephone.

As an additional help in spelling names correctly, keep a roster of the church membership close at hand as you compile the newsletter. Check all names against this official list. Update this file copy as new members join the church. It's a useful tool that can save hours of your valuable time.

Use a consistent style. Another detail that you should be concerned about is the literary style of your newsletter. Literary style refers to the unique way in which you capitalize, abbreviate, and punctuate certain words, phrases, and expressions that appear in your newsletter. When you use the phrase "Holy Communion," for example, is it capitalized or not? You need to make a decision about which style you will follow and stick with it consistently from issue to issue. Scores of words and phrases like these are used frequently in church newsletters. A good style guide will give you direction on how these expressions should appear in print.

An Easy-Reference Style Guide for Newsletter Editors is included in this book as chapter 12. Use this list as a place to begin in developing a consistent style for your newsletter.

Adopt a goal of compiling a style guide that is tailored to your newsletter's unique needs.

Proofread each issue carefully. Proofreading is the tedious process of reading back over your copy after you have typed it to make sure it contains no typographical errors. This is one of those picky detail jobs that can drive you up the wall, but it is absolutely essential for a first-class newsletter. It's amazing how many errors can creep into the copy from the time you write it until it appears in print. Careful proofreading can keep these errors to a minimum.

You probably have your own favorite "typographical error" story. But did you hear the one about the "hillside pastor"? It seems the church choir was supposed to sing an anthem entitled "Into the Hills My *Master* Went." But the title that actually appeared in the church bulletin on Sunday morning was "Into the Hills My *Pastor* Went!" Everyone, including the pastor, had a good laugh. But the church bulletin typist made a silent vow to do a better job of proofreading the next week!

The toughest proofreading job of all is to check a typed stencil. The print is very faint against a dark background. Proofread slowly so you can check every word. Proofreading of typed copy that you arrange into paste-ups or scan by electronic stencil is a little easier. But it always helps to have a second reading. If possible, let another member of the church staff go over the copy after you have given it a careful check. Sometimes another person can catch errors that you tend to read right over because of your familiarity with the material.

When you type your own copy and reproduce the newsletter on your own church's equipment, you don't have to be all that fancy in your proofreading. Just mark the errors with some system that makes sense to you. But if you send the newsletter out for typesetting and printing, you'll need to use the standard proofreading marks that your printer understands.

A typeset article for a church newsletter, with typical errors and proofreading marks included, is reproduced on page 12. These symbols should cover most of the errors you find as you proofread. For a complete roster of proofreading marks and symbols, see the latest edition of the *Chicago Manual of Style.*

A good attitude, usable systems, and appropriate tools—these will get you off to a good start in editing a first-class church newsletter. But how often to publish and in what format? These, too, are important points to consider. Move on to the next chapter for a discussion of these questions.

Newsletter with Routine, Ho-Hum Approach

Newsletter with Sparkling, Creative Approach

IMPORTANT

PUBLICATION DEADLINES

Is your group having something that you want publicized in the VISITOR or KING'S BUSINESS (Sunday Bulletin)? Then you need to be aware of these deadlines.

All items for the VISITOR must be turned in to the office no later than 5:00 p.m. on Monday of the week before the event. Example: Your meeting in on October 29, 1981, the deadline would be 5:00 p.m., Monday, October 19, 1981.

All items for the KING'S BUSINESS must be turned in to Randy no later than the Wednesday evening worship hour preceeding the Sunday it needs to be published. Example: For the meeting on October 29, the deadline would be the worship hour on Wednesday, October 21.

Articles or necessary material should be in writing. Don't rely on someone's memory, please! Regular meetings will not be listed if they are not on the church calendar in the main office. When you help us by observing these deadlines, communication about all the church happenings will be much better.

Deadline Policy Statement

COMMONLY USED PROOFREADING MARKS

Meaning

The date for the autumn retreat for for singles of our church is fast approaching. It will be held October 12-14. We will leave Fri. evening at 7:00 from fellowship hall and return in time for evening services on Sunday night. Theme of the retreat is "Building Better Relationships. Retreat speakers and conference Leaders include Roger Hendricks, Carolyn Miles, and Michael Sanborn.

The cost for meals, lodging, and conference materials is $30.00. If the finances are a problem please contact Tony DeLoach, minister education, to check on the possibility of scholaship assistance. If childcare is a problem, we will also work with you to find a sitter for the weekend. We don't want anyone to miss this great opportunity for fellowship and learning.

delete the word, "for"

correct spelling of word

spell word out

use capital letters, F and H

begin new paragraph

insert closing quotation marks

use lower case letter, "l"

insert comma

insert the word, "of"

transpose "r" and "a"

insert space; break one word into two

close space; combine two words into one

Commonly Used Proofreading Marks

2
The Right Frequency and Format for Your Publication

How often should the newsletter be published? And what size should it be for the maximum in eye appeal, convenience, and effectiveness? These are two big questions that every church newsletter editor needs to face sooner or later. You may be issuing a monthly publication in a 5½x8½″ page size simply because that's the way you have always done it. But does this publishing schedule and format really fit your church's needs and give you the time you need to put together a first-class publication? These are some of the questions you should grapple with as you think about frequency and format.

Frequency of Publication

At least 90 percent of the church newsletters in existence are published either weekly or monthly. Each of these publishing schedules has its own particular rationale. And each has its good points as well as its limitations.

Weekly. Congregations that publish this often are usually large, so they have the financial means to fund a weekly publication. They usually have a diverse and active church program, offering something for all age groups. They feel that nothing short of a weekly newsletter can communicate all these concerns consistently to every member of the church. Generally, a weekly church newsletter revolves around the weekly day of worship, encouraging members to attend and reporting on statistics and other newsworthy events that take place during this time.

The big advantage of a weekly newsletter is its timeliness. It can promote church concerns on a weekly basis. Late-breaking developments can be publicized almost immediately to keep the church members thoroughly informed.

But the problem with a weekly newsletter is that it can become a routine and ho-hum exercise. If you edit a weekly, you know how it goes. You're so pressured just to meet the publishing deadline that you don't have time to plan interesting news features or work out an exciting page layout and design. Because of the time problem, many weeklies become "department" publications—they're filled with standing columns like "Remember Our Sick," "From the Pastor," "Calendar of Events," and "Welcome, New Members." The information under these headings changes from week to week, but the basic format remains the same.

Closely related to this problem is the matter of inadequate space. Most weeklies are limited to four pages because of the expense of publishing weekly and difficulty of filling more pages on such a rushed schedule. This means that routine church concerns always crowd out the special features that could make the paper more exciting.

Monthly. If you publish a monthly newsletter, you may be congratulating yourself for choosing this path rather than taking on all the hassle of a weekly schedule. In many ways, your job is easier. A monthly deadline gives you plenty of time to plan more creative content and put together a more attractive publication. You probably don't have to fight the "treadmill syndrome" like those who serve as weekly editors.

But before you get too puffed up with pride, think about what you're giving up by publishing monthly. Timeliness is the biggest loss. A monthly publishing cannot effectively promote the weekly events on the church calendar. The best you can do is to publish near the first of the month, including a calendar of all the events scheduled for the next four weeks. If extra meetings are called during the month, these must be promoted with announcements during worship services or a special mailing to all members of the church.

So the truth is that you as a monthly editor are no better or no worse off than your weekly colleagues. Both of you just happen to work under a different set of advantages and problems.

Publishing every other week. One logical answer to the problems of publishing either weekly or monthly is to issue your newsletter every other week. This schedule is frequent enough to be timely in promoting upcoming church events. And it could give you the breathing space you need to put more creative effort into your publication.

The best publication time for an every-other-week newsletter for most churches is midweek. For example, schedule the release date so church members will receive the newsletter on alternate Wednesdays or Thursdays. Each issue might contain a report on what happened during the two preceding Sundays (new members, attendance, etc.) as well as important announcements about church events for the next two weeks. It's an alternative that more and more churches are beginning to use.

If this schedule appeals to you, here are some things to consider before adopting it as a permanent arrangement:

- Remember that twice per month is not the same as every other week. A twice-per-month schedule means there will be three Sundays between issues of your newsletter in "fifth Sunday" months. You don't have this problem with an every-other-week publishing schedule.
- Plan to publish announcements about church activities in your weekly worship bulletin, particularly during each "off Sunday" when the newsletter wasn't issued during the preceding week.
- Check with your local post office before tampering with your newsletter's frequency of publication. Certain provisions in your postal permit must be changed before you can start issuing under a new schedule.

Creative combinations. There's really no reason why you have to be restricted to a weekly, a monthly, or an every-other-week schedule in publishing your newsletter. The best approach for your church might be a combination plan that puts together the advantages of two different schedules.

For example, one innovative church issues its newsletter, *The Flame,* under two different schedules and formats. These two publications are referred to affectionately by the church staff as "the small flame" and "the large flame" (see illustrations on p. 15). The first, an 8½x11, two-page publication, is issued every other week to promote the regular church program. It is brief, pointed, and factual in its approach. But "the large flame" is published four times per year in an impressive newspaper tabloid format (12x16" page size). It contains photographs, feature stories, and well-researched articles about interesting developments in the life of the church and its people.

Notice from the reproduction of "the large flame" how many different people wrote articles for this special issue of the newsletter. This is an excellent way to get creative members of your church involved in sharing their talents with fellow Christians. Artists and photographers could also be enlisted in a special project like this.

The Flame is a good case study in the combination approach to church newsletter publishing. Issuing the paper on two different schedules in widely diverse forms allows this church to be factual and timely as well as interesting, creative, and people-centered with its publication.

One variation on the combination approach is to make an occasional issue of your newsletter extra special. For example, if you publish weekly, plan to double or triple the number of pages in your paper at least once per quarter. Fill these extra pages with essays, features, photos, and special articles written by members of your church. Some churches do this regularly and use the special issue in membership recruitment. It's an ideal promotional piece to mail to all residents of the community or to all visitors for the past sev-

eral months who have shown an interest in the church. Careful long-range planning is essential for such special issues of the newsletter.

Just to be sure, check with your local post office before planning any special issues or any combination publishing schedules for your newsletter. Make the necessary changes in your postal permit in advance so you won't have any problems at mailing time.

So much for how often your newsletter should be published. Now let's look at another important question—the right page size and format for the church paper.

Page Size and Format

Most church newsletters are printed on 8½x11" or 8½x14" (legal size) sheets of paper. Inexpensive paper stock in many colors in these two convenient sizes is readily available in most locations. This is probably the main reason why churches continue to use these familiar sheet sizes for their publications.

But you may have never thought about the many different page sizes and formats that can be formed from these two common sheets of paper. Take a careful look at the illustrations on pages 16-17. They show two different page sizes that can be formed from 8½x11" paper and four different newsletter formats that are possible with 8½x14" paper. To simplify our discussion, we'll refer to these different formats by the numbers—1 through 6.

The path of least resistance in newsletter publishing is to adopt the sheet size as the page size—to arrange your copy page for page after the format dictated by the 8½x11" or the 8½x14" sheets of paper. This is the approach used in formats 1 and 3. Both these formats yield newsletters of two pages each—printed front and back on these standard-size sheets of paper.

But formats 2, 4, 5, and 6 show more creativity in their layout and design. The copy is arranged on these sheets in such a way that they form attractive newsletters of either four or six pages each when printed and folded. A church paper divided into convenient pages like these just seems to come across with more of an "official publication" image.

One of the most attractive formats in this series is #5. This six-page newsletter is formed by printing three pages, front and back, on a legal-size sheet of paper, then folding the sheet twice. The result is a compact publication that's divided into three equal panels of two pages each. It's a dream to handle, mail, and read.

One variation on this approach is format #6. This 8½x14" sheet of paper is also folded twice—but in such a fashion that one of the three sections is only 3" wide. This little "pop-out panel" is an ideal place for printing a tabular listing, such as the weekly schedule of church events, birthdays of church members, or a statistical report.

Many other page sizes and formats are possible for your newsletter, particularly if you have it reproduced by a local printer. One option that seems to be growing in popularity among larger congregations is the tabloid newspaper format. Paper cost is a big factor if you publish frequently and have a big circulation. If you print as many as five thousand copies per issue, you might look into the tabloid format as a possibility for your church.

Now that you have considered the right frequency and format for your newsletter, let's get down to some specifics about editorial content. This important subject is explored in chapter 3.

"Small Flame"—
Published Every Other Week:
Pointed, Factual, Program-Oriented

"Large Flame"—Published Once Every Three Months:
Creative, Interesting, People-Oriented

16

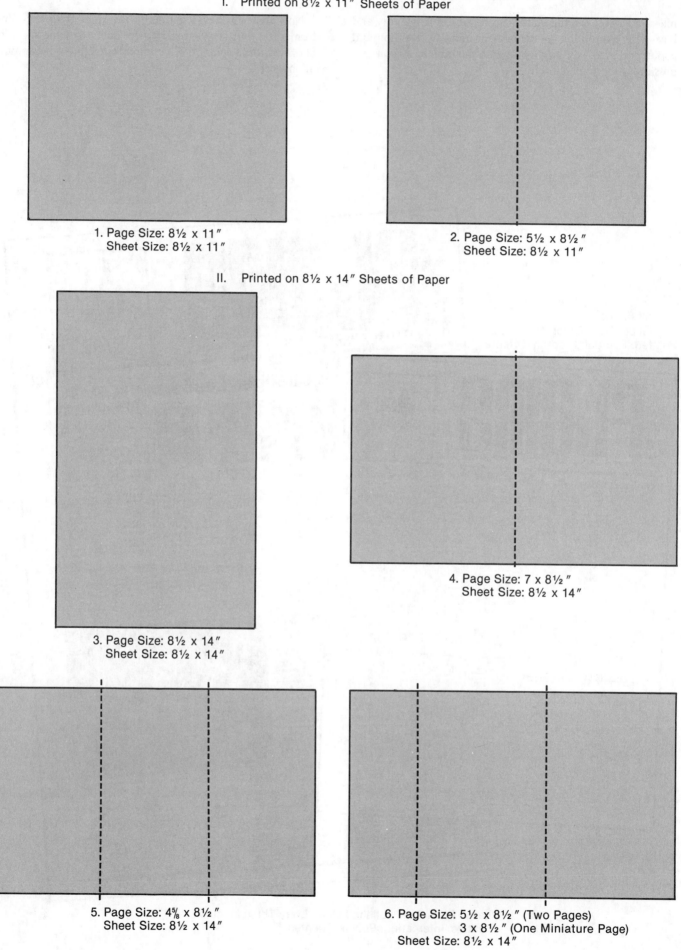

I. Printed on 8½ x 11″ Sheets of Paper

1. Page Size: 8½ x 11″
Sheet Size: 8½ x 11″

2. Page Size: 5½ x 8½″
Sheet Size: 8½ x 11″

II. Printed on 8½ x 14″ Sheets of Paper

3. Page Size: 8½ x 14″
Sheet Size: 8½ x 14″

4. Page Size: 7 x 8½″
Sheet Size: 8½ x 14″

5. Page Size: 4⅝ x 8½″
Sheet Size: 8½ x 14″

6. Page Size: 5½ x 8½″ (Two Pages)
3 x 8½″ (One Miniature Page)
Sheet Size: 8½ x 14″

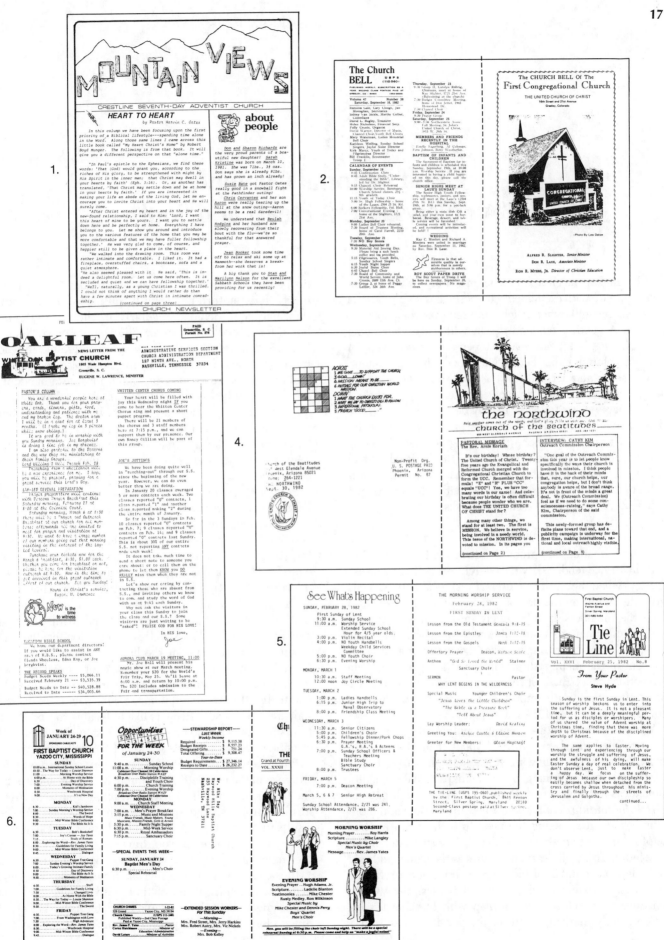

3
Good Editorial Content:
Your Newsletter's Heart and Soul

What makes one church newsletter deadly dull while another sparkles with excitement? In most cases it's a matter of editorial content—what articles and features you choose to publish. A good layout and design will make your paper more exciting, but it can never compensate for weak copy. A first-class church paper begins with good editorial content.

And here's another truth just as important: The purpose of a newsletter dictates the type of material it publishes. A church paper exists for three clearly defined reasons: (1) to keep members informed about the programs, ministries, and activities of the church, (2) to strengthen the fellowship of the congregation, and (3) to nurture the spiritual growth of every member of the church. Let's look at these three purposes of the church newsletter, along with some of the specific features that grow out of these tasks.

Information

The information and promotion function is the most important service rendered by the church newsletter. Gone are the days when the church could make a few announcements from the pulpit on the day of worship and expect these to keep the membership adequately informed. The typical church today may have several events going on at the same time, each targeted to a specialized age group or a different segment of the membership. The church paper is the one promotional tool that reaches every member consistently week after week with important news about *all* the programs and activities of the congregation.

What are some features you can publish in your newsletter to keep members informed about their church's life and ministry? The following list is not exhaustive, but it does serve as a beginning point. Perhaps it will generate some ideas for similar features in your own church paper.

Helpful routine details about the church. More and more churches are recognizing the need to include routine but helpful information about the church in every issue of the newsletter. This includes such features as the name, address, and telephone number of the church; roster of church staff members; a statement of theological beliefs; the weekly schedule of church services; a map with the church's location clearly marked; layout of the parking areas; and a list of the rooms where the various Sunday School classes meet. This material is usually published as "standing information"—included regularly in the newsletter and boxed for special emphasis (see illustrations on p. 23).

These features show that a church is interested in reaching new people for membership. They also increase the usability of the newsletter, making it ideal as a handout or mailout to prospective new members. Remember, too, that marginal members may forget your church's schedule and the meeting places of their Sunday School classes. The newsletter's task is to keep *all* members informed—not just those who have been members for years and who attend faithfully every week.

Summary of church statistics. One of the most popular features in church newsletters of all denominations is an ongoing statistical summary of attendance at worship services and Sunday School, amount given through tithes and offerings, and new members who have affiliated with the church. This is a good standing feature to keep members informed about the ebb and flow of congregational life.

One church has expanded this basic idea (see illustration, p. 24) to include baptisms, marriages, and deaths among the membership. It publishes all this information together in its monthly newsletter under the heading "Parish Concerns." Church members can turn to this page for a quick review of this important information each month. If you publish a feature like this, try to put it on the same page or in the same spot issue after issue. Readers like to be able to find this information quickly and conveniently, just as they turn to the classified ads or the sports section of the daily newspaper.

Promotion of major church events. One of the most effective roles of the newsletter is to publicize important events in the life of the church—revivals, training courses, retreats, mission projects, and special worship services. For best results in promoting big events like these, start early, use a variety of approaches as you draw closer to the event, and then follow up to let church members know what happened.

In the case of a church revival, for example, you might begin two months ahead of time with a small boxed announcement about the event and the date. As the kickoff day draws closer, you could publish an article about the guest speaker, a letter from the pastor about his hopes for the revival, and testimonies from two or three members about how they plan to support this important church project. Finally, after the event is over, a brief article in the newsletter could report on its results in the life of the church.

The personal testimony is a powerful promotional technique. People will listen to their fellow church members who speak out of their own experience and sense of commitment. But newsletters have been slow to use this method to promote church events, perhaps because of the space which printed testimonies require. The example from one newsletter (see illustration, p. 24) shows that testimonies don't have to be long to be effective. These brief, positive statements from church members about a training opportunity were used to encourage others to sign up for the course.

Follow-up promotion is another technique which newsletters seldom use. But why expend hundreds of words to publicize a big event, only to forget it the minute it's over? The congregation has a right to know what happened. The article from one newsletter about a youth hunger project (see illustration, p. 25) shows some of the possibilities of good follow-up promotion. This excellent report had the very practical effect of making the rest of the church more aware of the problem of world hunger.

Enlistment of volunteers. In addition to promoting church events, the newsletter is also an effective tool for enlisting volunteers for specific church projects. Some congregations do this effectively by publishing appeals for volunteers, accompanied by clip-out commitment forms which members complete and turn in to indicate their willingness to serve (see illustration, p. 25). This is an excellent way to recruit volunteers for specialized or short-term projects.

Report on official church actions. Most churches have an orderly system for carrying on its work, whether through a "business meeting," an official board, or some other decision-making body. One of the greatest services the newsletter can render is to publish a full report on the actions taken at these official meetings. It's amazing how many rumors can circulate about the "decisions" of the deliberating group if members don't have all the facts. The best way to combat these half-truths is to make sure the rest of the church is fully informed. This should be done through the newsletter as quickly as possible after the actions are taken.

The report could be written by the moderator, the presiding officer, or some member of the church staff who is always present for these official meetings. Or you could compile it yourself from your own notes or the official minutes recorded by the clerk or administrative secretary. The article from a newsletter entitled "Administrative Board" (see illustration, p. 26) could serve as a model for your own report. Notice that the tone of this feature is official and direct. This is not the place for cute comments and subjective interpretations of the actions that were taken. The newsletter's job is to report the facts.

Missions awareness features. Churches with a well-balanced program don't expend all their time and money on themselves. They are involved in meeting needs of the larger world beyond their own communities. Congregations do this in a number of ways. They may help the poor through a local benevolence committee, contribute to their denomination's foreign missions effort, or send out youth as summer missionaries. One of your most challenging jobs as newsletter editor is to *personalize* these various mission efforts for every member of the church. They need to realize that they have an important supporting role in these worthwhile projects, although they may not be directly involved.

The illustrations on page 27 show some creative possibilities for such missions awareness promotion in church newsletters. The article "Know Your Chapels" informs members about the several different mission churches which one congregation sponsors throughout its city. "Missionary Prayer Concern of the Week" is a feature article which appears in every issue of another church paper. It focuses on a different missionary family or missions concern which this church helps to sponsor through regular contributions to its denominational mission board. And "A Summer of Ministry" is a report from a teenager about her work as a counselor in a day camp sponsored by her church.

Notice how each of these features takes the abstract idea of *missions* and translates it into real people, places, and projects that the congregation can identify with. This is the secret of effective missions awareness promotion through the newsletter.

Stewardship promotion. Another area of church life that deserves good promotion through the newsletter is stewardship. Unless members support their church financially, money for missions and other worthy projects will not be available.

The foundation of the stewardship program of any church is total openness and honesty about the way all contributions are spent. The newsletter is an ideal place for publishing periodic financial reports that list all income and expenditures in detail (see illustration, p. 28). When the congregation or administrative board approves a new budget at the beginning of the church year, this should also be printed in full in the newsletter for thorough review and analysis by all members of the church.

Other stewardship promotion features for the church paper include articles on the total amount pledged in special fund drives (see illustration, p. 28) and front-page "celebration announcements" (see illustration, p. 29) when the church buys a new piece of property or pays off the note on one of its buildings. Marking these occasions through the newsletter can help generate enthusiasm for the financial priorities of the church.

Church library promotion. A treasury of good books and study material is available to church members through the library. What a tragedy that so many don't know about it or refuse to take advantage of its services! Use your church newsletter to correct this situation. Publicize the hours when the library is open so people will know when to drop by. Publish an occasional feature article like one church paper did to reinforce the library's usefulness as a resource center (see illustration, p. 30).

Better still, include a book review column as a regular feature in the newsletter (see illustration, p. 30). Ask the church librarian for the names of members who check out books regularly. Then follow up and ask these people to provide short reviews of the books they read for publication. Many will be glad to do this as a service to others. Publish their names with the reviews as an extra incentive. With a little planning and creativity, you can use the newsletter to make the library a more useful servant of the church.

Sunday School promotion. If your church has a Sunday School or Church School with classes for all age groups, use your newsletter to promote this important ministry. Chances are your church's most loyal members attend the Sunday School. Through the newsletter you can encourage all members of the church to get involved in this ministry.

Why not publish an occasional preview of the upcoming Sunday School lesson in the church paper? (See illustration, p. 31.) Another approach is to publish personality profiles on specific teachers or to focus on different age groups or departments of the Church School from issue to issue (see illustrations, p. 31). Published several times during the year, these articles can serve as reminders to all members of the importance of Bible study.

Specialized ministry focus. One problem in churches today is that members are not aware of the many specialized ministries which their congregations may be sponsoring. The newsletter should take the initiative to focus on these ministries to keep the membership informed. The feature article on a church's radio broadcast ministry (see illustration, p. 32) appeared in one forward-looking newsletter. Other specialized ministries that could be profiled like this include a food and clothing bank for the needy, counseling services, work with language or ethnic groups, and so forth.

The possibilities are endless when it comes to promoting the church program through the newsletter. Keeping the members informed about all the worthwhile ministries and activities of the modern church can take all your time unless you remember that the church paper has other duties to perform. One of the most important is to enrich the fellowship of the church.

Fellowship

Years ago, when life was simple and churches were small, no one had to be too concerned about the quality of a congregation's fellowship. Most of the members knew one another. This spirit of familiarity and camaraderie spilled over into the corporate life of the church, enriching the relationships of members and drawing them all closer together.

But all that changed with the suburban boom, the breakdown of community life, and the high mobility rate of our society. Churches today are made up of people who are strangers to one another—except for the common bond which they share in their faith. This means that one of the most important parts of your job is to use the newsletter to enrich fellowship. This includes everything from recognizing people for their individual accomplishments to helping church members get to know one another better. The following suggested features for your church paper should get you started in this direction.

Welcome to new members. A "Welcome, New Members" feature, complete with photos, if possible, can help these newcomers get off to a good start in your church. This feature also helps church members of long standing get to know these new people a little better. The example from one church newsletter (see illustration, p. 32) shows the technique of publishing photos and names as well as the addresses of all new members. This encourages church members to write cards or letters to add their own personal words of welcome to these new members of the fellowship.

Warm, personal items about members. People are attracted·to a church that is warm and personal. Make sure your newsletter includes features that generate these feelings. One proven way to establish this mood is to include a column about significant events in people's lives—awards received, marriages, births, deaths, retirements, graduations, honors, recognitions, etc. One sensitive pastor does this through his regular column in the church paper (see illustration, p. 32). Or you could publish these brief news notes under their own column heading. "Church Chatter," "Among the Membership," or "Our Members in the News" are some title possibilities for such a column.

Other newsletter features that establish a warm, personal mood are a "Happy Birthday" column, a "Baby of the Week" feature, and expressions of thanks to the church and individual members (see illustrations, p. 33). Notice the expressions of thanks can be handled as individual letters, or they can be published in abbreviated form under a "Thank You" column head. No matter how it's said, "thank you" always portrays a friendly, caring church.

Recognition for church accomplishments. Another good way to enrich church fellowship is to recognize accomplishments of the members through articles in the newsletter. One church, for example, listed the names of boys and girls who participated in a Scripture memory project (see illustration, p. 35). This type of recognition takes little space, and it cultivates a healthy sense of accomplishment and team spirit among the entire membership. Appropriate recognition for significant accomplishments could also be given occasionally through the church paper to other segments of the church.

Feature focus on individuals or groups. What could be more appropriate for your newsletter than an occasional feature article that focuses on interesting persons or specialized groups in the church? Church members who read the two articles of this type in their newsletters (see illustrations, pp. 34-35) must have been impressed with the creative diversity of their respective congregations. Good features like these can help the church understand the contributions which many people and groups are making to its total ministry.

"Just-for-fun" material. Finally, enrich the fellowship of your church by publishing cartoons, humorous essays, and other light features in your newsletter occasionally. One church did this effectively by printing a full-page announcement about its annual "No-Excuses, Not-for-Men-Only" golf tournament (see illustration, p. 36). The detail in the fine print of this announcement is a case study in good humorous writing. Church people need to get together occasionally for some good, fellowship-enriching fun. This newsletter did the church a real service by promoting the tournament in a light and humorous vein.

Spiritual Nurture

In addition to promotion and fellowship-building, the newsletter also exists to enrich the faith of church members. Too many people never grow in their faith. They fail to see how it relates in a practical way to the problems, issues, and circumstances of life. A good church newsletter should challenge this type of mentality. Some of its editorial content should be devoted to the spiritual growth and nurture of the members of the church. Perhaps some of the following suggested features will help you do this with your own newsletter.

Inspiration and encouragement. Church members are often discouraged by circumstances and their own failures as they try to live the Christian life. Speak to this need through the newsletter by publishing short, inspirational articles that are designed to strengthen and encourage—Bible verses, uplifting thoughts and quotations, and thought-provoking fillers (see illustrations, p. 36). Items like these have a way of lifting your readers' spirits at the moments when they need it most.

Reinforcement of pulpit ministry. One goal of the preaching of most ministers is to nurture the faith of church members. This means you can contribute to the spiritual development of the church by reinforcing the preaching ministry through the newsletter at every opportunity. Why not use the church paper to publicize a special series of sermons, to announce the fall preaching schedule, or even to print an outstanding sermon in full, if space is available? (See illustrations, p. 37.) These are excellent ways to enlarge the preaching ministry of the church and challenge church members to a deeper faith at the same time.

Insights into personal needs. In the age of "pop psychology," every talk show seems to feature a therapist with an instant answer to all our problems. Churches need to show there's a difference between the easy answers advocated by so many and the authentic answer that is grounded in faith. And what better place for a good, solid counseling column than the pages of your newsletter? More and more churches are publishing such features to offer their readers insights into common problems like depression, anger, poor self-esteem, and broken relationships. The article on depression from one church newsletter (see illustration, p. 38) demonstrates the possibilities of a regular column like this for your own church paper.

A forum on vital issues. What does the Christian faith have to say about such current moral issues as abortion, medical ethics, world hunger, and politics? The answer is, *Plenty.* And one way to show that it does is to open the pages of your newsletter to church members who want to speak their minds on these topics. The essay on television entitled "Holiness and Hollywood" (see illustration, p. 39) was written by one church member for publication in his church paper.

A variation on the one-article approach might be to mention a moral issue such as capital punishment in one issue of the newsletter. Invite church members to express their opinions on this topic in the form of "letters to the editor." All their responses could be published in the next issue of the church paper.

Wouldn't it be interesting to see how church members themselves apply their faith to some of the tough problems of contemporary life? Try it. It's guaranteed to increase readership of your newsletter by several percentage points.

Other Content Possibilities

Information, fellowship, and spiritual nurture. Remember these three purposes of the newsletter, and they will help you select material that is right on target. But don't limit your content to these three areas alone. Some of the most creative church papers include features that can't be neatly categorized under any of these three purposes. Put your mind in the creative mode as you read over the following possibilities. Some of these may be ideal for your own newsletter.

Special literary/arts issue. Why not give one issue of your newsletter every year a literary and artistic bent? Promote this project well in advance. Invite members of your church to submit their poems, essays, paintings, and drawings for publication in this special edition. You might also publish the newsletter in connection with a churchwide arts and crafts festival, where all the creative skills of your membership can be displayed—sewing, ceramics, sculpture, photography, etc. The newsletter could publish as many of these creative works as possible and include articles on all the items contained in the exhibit.

Something for the children. Most church papers are directed to the adult members of the church. But why not include an occasional feature just for the children? Kids love puzzles and word games. One church published a "Bible Jumbles" game to get the children involved in an interesting activity that would also teach the names of books of the Bible (see illustration, p. 40).

Another way to spark the children's interest is to sponsor an art contest (see illustration, p. 40). Winning entries could be published in the newsletter. One creative church asked the children to write letters to God as part of an educational activity. These letters were then published in the church paper to show all members of the church what the children were learning (see illustration, p. 40). All these are good techniques for getting the church's younger set more involved in the newsletter.

A recipe feature. In most churches members are always asking one another for favorite recipes. Why not formalize this custom and provide a needed service by publishing a recipe feature? (See illustration, p. 41.) Ask the outstanding chefs of your church to submit their best recipes for publication. After you have published these recipes for a couple of years, you might want to pull them all together into a handy pamphlet or book for distribution to all interested members.

Information gathering. The newsletter is an ideal medium for gathering needed information from church members. One church paper, for example, published a "WMU Mission Action Survey," directed to all the women of the church (see illustration, p. 41). Its purpose was to discover those who would use their skills to get involved in special mission projects in the community.

You could use this same technique to take a talent and skills inventory among the total membership for the purpose of leadership recruitment. Or ask church members to turn in the names of those who might be interested in affiliating with your church. Don't overlook the value of your church paper as an information-gathering tool.

Denominational and religious news. Finally, if you publish frequently and have the space, you might consider scheduling a column of general religious news or news about your denomination for your church paper. Your newsletter is the one contact that many of your readers have with your denomination or the Christian world in general. An abbreviated section of such news, like that published by one newsletter (see illustration, p. 41), would be a real service to them.

Most denominations have their own news or public relations services that gather and distribute news about the work of their respective groups. Contact this agency for your denomination to subscribe to its news service. For information and prices on general religious news subscription services, write to Religious News Service, 43 W. 57th St., New York, New York 10019 and Evangelical News Service, P.O. Box 4550, Overland Park, Kansas 66204.

By now you should be convinced of the endless possibilities for good editorial content for your newsletter. But what the church paper contains is only the beginning of the search for excellence. Good design is also essential for a first-class publication. This subject is explored in the next chapter.

Services At Calvary Baptist

	NORTH	SOUTH
Sunday School	9:30 a.m.	10:50 a.m.
Morning Worship Service	10:50 a.m.	9:30 a.m.
Evening Service	6:00 p.m.	6:00 p.m.
Prayer Meeting	Wednesday, 7:00 p.m.	
Church Calling	Thursday, 7:00 p.m.	

We have classes for all ages. The following is a general guide which you can use to select a class where you can feel most at home.

AGE	CLASS
Single College & Early Career	College/Career
Single Adults in Professions	Professional
Married 7 years or less	Alpha
Under 40, Married over 7 years	Torchlighters
40-50	Crusaders
50-60	Conquerors
60 and up	Maranatha and Esther

STATEMENT OF BELIEFS

We are a group of Bible-believing Christians who gather for the purpose of worshipping and bringing glory to our Father in heaven. We believe that this can best be accomplished through a ministry of Bible teaching, leadership training, and outreach service for the Lord.

We believe the fundamental doctrines of historic Baptist Christianity, including the Divine inspiration of the Bible, the person of the Holy Spirit, and the Deity of Jesus Christ; His Virgin birth, substitutionary death, bodily resurrection and visible second coming.

We further believe in a literal, historical and grammatical interpretation of the Word of God; placing God's Word at the center of a believer's life.

First Baptist Church
11704 Kingston Pike
Concord Station
Knoxville, TN 37922

CALVARY'S PARKING MAP

Pictured are four major parking areas surrounding Calvary Baptist Church. We are asking that as many of Calvary's members as possible commit to parking in one of the four areas freeing City Hall and EB 3 lots for senior citizens, handicapped and visitors. Thank you for your cooperation!

SUNDAY SCHOOL DIRECTORY

Bedbabies	S-1&3	3rd Grade	S-23
Creepers	S-5&7	3rd Grade	S-26
Toddlers A	S-9	4th Grade	S-21
Toddlers B	S-2	4th Grade	S-24
Toddlers C	S-4	Exceptional	N-6
2 Year Old A	S-6	5th & 6th Grades	N-31
2 Year Old B	S-8	7th Grade	E-1
2 Year Old C	S-10	8th Grade	E-2
3 Year Olds	S-12	9th Grade	E-3
3 Year Olds	S-14	High School	S. W. Cafeteria
3 Year Olds	S-16	College & Career (C-22)	N-21
4 Year Olds	S-18	Adult I (Young Singles 23-34)	N-23
4 Year Olds	S-25	Adult II (Young Marrieds M-26)	N-22
5 Year Olds	N-3	Adult III (Bereans 27-40)	N-25, 26, 27, 29
5 Year Olds	N-5	Adult IV (41-52)	N-24
1st Grade	N-7	Adult V (Men 53-64)	N-2
1st Grade	N-9	Adult V (Women 53-58)	N-4
2nd Grade	S-28	Adult V (Women 59-64)	N-14
2nd Grade	S-30	Adult VI (65-up)	N-1
		Pastor's Class	Auditorium

Helpful, Routine Information Published Regularly in Newsletter

Parish Concerns

BAPTISMS:

TIMOTHY KIRK NELSON, born 4/8/82, son of Mr. & Mrs. Kirk Nelson (Bridget)

ALISSA MARIA LEON, born 11/13/73, daughter of Mrs. Susan Leon and the late Ramon Leon

LAURA MARIE VANDENBURGH, born 5/19/82, daughter of Mr. & Mrs. David Vandenburgh (Julie)

SCOTT MITCHELL CUSHMAN, born 6/18/82, son of Mr. & Mrs. Glenn Cushman (Susan)

JENNIFER RUTH JONES (adult)

ROBERT WILLIAM SCHMITT (adult)

ANN MICHELE WEBBER (adult)

PAUL MARSHALL WEBBER (adult)

CORBIN BOONE WRIGHT (adult)

MARRIAGES:

Kevin Ganam & Kathryn Dobberphul

Robert Danely & Terri Milton

Douglas Miller & Jean Godwin

Ted Allyn & Stacie Zimmerman

Albert Giesecke & Renate Lewis

DEATHS:

Ida Sells
Mary Rominger
Bessie Renfro
Ruth Scheible
Alma Holmes Neal

NEW MEMBERS FROM MAY 30, 1982

Michael Brewer
Ms. Beverly Carroll
Mr. & Mrs. Jack Eberenz (Heidi)
Mrs. Aderine Ebner
Mr. & Mrs. Bernard Garmire (Elizabeth)
Ms. Mary Lou Hapner

Mr. & Mrs. Don Hough (Linda)
Mr. & Mrs. Gerald Jones (Ruth)
Mr. & Mrs. Alan Le Win (Dorothy)
Ms. Gail O'Connor
Ms. Gene Sanders

The next class of New Members will be received into the church on September 26. Those interested in joining please contact the church office...

Church Statistics
Summary Page

EVANGELISM EXPLOSION
LEARN HOW TO WIN SOULS

OUR SPRING SCHEDULE (14 WEEKS OF TRAINING)

ADULT E.E. TRAINING BEGINS SUNDAY, JAN. 31
Sun. evenings-5:15-6:45pm (Classroom Training)
Tues.evenings-6:30-8:30pm (O.J.T.On the Job Training)

YOUTH E.E. TRAINING BEGINS SATURDAY, JAN.30
Sat.- 9:30-11:00-(Classroom Training)
11:00- 1:00-(O.J.T.-On the Job Training)

"...E.E. shows me just how hungry the world is and how much more we as Christians need to make sure they hear the answer in Jesus." Susan Price

"...it provided me with a clear Gospel presentation mode." John Chaloupka

"E.E. means growing in Christ, sharing Christ and excitement of seeing others come to know Him." Gerri Danielson

"...E.E. is so basic I can share it with children." G. Atkins

"...it has given me a boldness and better understanding of my own witness & responsibility as a Christian." -Vicki Alexander

"...it has been the Gospel in action in my life." Tom Burnett

"E.E. has helped make me comfortable in sharing the Gospel." Bill Sawyer

"...it has been a big instrument in the growth of my personal relationship with God." Billy Allen

"...I can now share the wonderful Gospel in a meaningful way. My priorities in life have changed completely..." Juanita Morris

"E.E.has taught me to share the Gospel even when I don't have my Bible with me." James Welch

"It helps provide the right words with good Scripture verses to back it up." Joy Hardwick

Effective Promotion with Personal Testimonies

30 HOURS WITHOUT FOOD

"Let It Growl" Report

June 19, 1981 11:30 AM Famine Begins—June 20, 1981 5:30 PM Famine Ends

That's 30 hours without food! Seven teenagers—Beth Eppinger, Betsy Henry, Rob Jones, Kelly Roman, Jennifer Walz, Jennifer Jordan, and Audrey Silver, and sponsor, Tom Close, participated in a truly profound and enlightening experience.

Why did we do it? What good did it do? Would we do it again? These were a few of the questions we got; and here are some answers...

WHY? Because we are sincerely concerned about world hunger and just raising money was not enough. We had to experience hunger to fully understand the frustration of hungry people.

WHAT GOOD DID IT DO? We raised over $360.00 to be used to feed hungry people, but more than that, we now have a greater appreciation of our blessings and the food we have to eat. We studied hungry people; the children dying of malnutrition and the parents crying because they are unable to provide for them. Now we can no longer sit down to a meal and not be reminded of how very much these children would want to eat just a part of our meal. We called it Christian Compassion.

WOULD WE DO IT AGAIN? Even before the famine was over, the kids were planning one for next year, only we want more people to participate so they could come to know this feeling of Christian Compassion as we came to know it.

WHAT DID WE DO FOR 30 HOURS? We saw movies, studied food shortage causes, talked about ways we could help, played tennis and other games, and just enjoyed each others company. A WONDERFUL EXPERIENCE!

HOW DID WE FEEL AT THE END? Empty—weak—drained of energy—tired and hungry.

But the real story in all of this is not us, it's the millions of hungry people all over the world, for they are still suffering, and still [...] out of our sight doesn't mean they should [...] prayer and sacrifice is required if we're [...] ese people. So now that we have finished [...] there are still hungry people throughout

[...] ers and to the outstanding young people [...] onal sacrifice.

Tom Close

[...] ust Newsletter is July 19th. The newsletter [...] d Sunday of each month.

Follow-Up Report on Church Event

V.B.S. Workers

If you would be interested in working in Vacation Bible School this year, June 7-11 please call the church office or fill out this and drop it in the offering plate on Sunday.

Yes, I would like to serve in Vacation Bible School.

Name_____

Phone_____

I prefer to work with:
____ Gen.Officers   ____ 1st grade
____ 2 yr. olds   ____ 2nd grade
____ 3 yr. olds   ____ 3rd grade
____ 4 yr. olds   ____ 4th grade
____ 5 yr. olds   ____ 5th grade
                         ____ 6th grade

Recruiting Volunteers with Clip-Out Forms

ADMINISTRATIVE BOARD

The Administrative Board met on October 5 at 8:00 P.M. with 18 present. Minutes of September 14 meeting was read and approved. Eugene Bell, Church Treasurer, presented a written report which was accepted. Pastor Walz presented a written pastor's report which was discussed.

Tom Grove, Chairman of Council on Ministries, announced the following events for October:
1. Finance Committee will meet on October 7.
2. Sub-District Revival will be held each night from October 11-18.
3. There will be a Prayer Vigil on October 17 from 8:00 A.M.-7:00 P.M. for the upcoming LWM.
4. Pastor-Parish Committee will meet on October 20.
5. Pastor-Parish Training Session will be October 21.
6. Lay Witness Mission will be held October 23,24,25.
7. Council on Ministries will meet on October 26.
8. There will be a Halloween Party at the Church on October 31 from 7:00 P.M.-9:00 P.M.

The Council on Ministries recommended a children's pamplet be given to the children staying for church. This will be on a trial basis. The recommendation was seconded by Bernie Jones.

Jim Redick, Chairman of Trustees, announced the Education Committee had separated some of the Sunday School classes and started another class. Four sheets of celetex will be purchases for classes needing bulletin boards. Herb Eppinger will be in charge of drawing up the plans for the landscaping for the new parsonage. The plan will be presented in the spring.

Don Clark will be paid $3,298.00 for the carpet in the new parsonage. The cost for the brick will be approximately $4,700.00.

Madeline Dunham asked permission to use the Church basement on October 6 for a DAR meeting. Debbie Haines also asked permission to have a meeting in the Church basement on October 21.

Meeting was adjourned at 8:30 P.M. Next Board meeting will be on November 2 at 7:30 P.M.

KNOW YOUR CHAPELS

MEADOW GARDENS CHAPEL

This chapel is located in Oak Cliff at 2902 McGowan St. The church now reaches portions of the Anglo, Mexican-American, and black population of the area with its program.

Meadow Gardens Chapel, through its bus ministry, has quite a wide outreach into this area of the city. They drive several miles of bus routes, picking up people for their services. They also have placed special emphasis upon Vacation Bible Schools and neighborhood outreach Bible schools as a means of meeting the needs of boys and girls in the area who are not already involved in any other church.

Please pray for this chapel as we seek a new pastor to lead this work. The potential is great to reach lost people for Christ.

Lanny Elmore,
Minister of Outreach

A Summer of Ministry

by D'Anne Hall

June 10 - September 4: Summer vacation. What would the Lord want me to do for those weeks? ...

... horses are so tall!

Swimming is a favorite summer pastime, and that comes on Wednesday. Gunn Lake is a great place to spend a hot, humid day! And then it's back to the park on Thursday for arts and crafts. On Friday we wind up the week with a surprise activity and a cookout.

... each day includes a storytime and Bible verse time. This summer we have been studying ... Animal Kingdom. The campers have been learning about character qualities such as responsibility, loyalty and ... ge through the behavior ... animals. We then look to ... ure for lessons on these ... character qualities in ... . As I have worked with ... stories, I have come to ... importance of building ... er at an early age. The ... and correlated Bible ... ave been an excellent ... eaching children about ... e of character God ... or their lives.

... ime is the part of the ... deserves special atten- ... campers work on two ... each day, Monday ... Thursday. On Friday ... ewarded if they have ... d all eight verses, ... many of the children achieve this goal.

During verse time, the counselor works with his or her team as a group to introduce the verses and briefly explain them. Then each child finds a shady tree and continues to drill alone. This is where lives are ...

... changed at Adventure Day Camp and children's souls are brought into God's kingdom. The counselor is able to spend time alone with each child during this part of the day presenting the plan of salvation or exhorting a Christian to a closer walk or discussing some problems in the child's life. This one-to-one relationship enables the child to ask questions and express feelings he never would in a group. It also encourages him to think about areas of his life that he might wish to avoid. Verse time is invaluable. I see it as the best part of the day because of the results it produces.

Within the first six weeks of Day Camp, twenty-one children prayed to receive Christ as their personal Savior. In others we have observed genuine attitude changes. We have seen many begin to display character qualities which are pleasing to Christ.

As I stated earlier, my reason for working with Adventure Day Camp was that it would be a challenge and a good place of spiritual ministry. It has not ceased to be a challenge! The Lord has something exciting planned in every day. There are always new questions to be asked, new problems to solve, new experiences from which the campers. . .and counselors . . .can learn. The summer has passed quickly and yet it has been rewarding to see the Lord work in children's lives.

MISSIONARY PRAYER CONCERN OF THE WEEK
David & Charlotte Etheridge

David and Charlotte are involved in a church planting ministry with the Bible Christian Union (BCU) in the Republic of Ireland. Their ministry is located in the city of Dundalls which is near the border of Northern Ireland. Dundalls is a city of 30,000 but David estimates that there are only about 50 born again Christians living in the city. He and Charlotte are ministering through a newly organized Baptist church. They hope to move into a church building where the congregation has died out to only one member.

Let us remember to lift up these servants of the Lord. Ireland and Northern Ireland are the scenes of much bloodshed and violence. Pray that the deep bitterness and resentments may be healed by a mighty turning of the people to the Lord. Pray for God's protection upon David and Charlotte in that they represent a small minority of evangelical believers in a country which is openly opposed to Protestants. Finally, pray that the small group of evangelical believers they minister to will be revived and become effective witnesses to the lost in Ireland. Remember, when you give your Faith Promise Offering to the World Missions Program you are part of reaching Ireland with the Word!

Reaching the world with the Word

... through group games, relays and individual races at a local park. Tuesday is the highlight of the week for some children. That is the day for horseback riding. Often it's the first time for campers and they are surprised that the ...

Three Different Missions Awareness Features

28

FIRST BAPTIST CHURCH — JANUARY, 1982 — FINANCIAL STATEMENT

Cash in Bank — December 31, 1981

RECEIPTS:

Unified Budget	$13,042
Designated Gifts	$42,481
Child Enrichment Center	2,320
TOTAL RECEIPTS	8,231
	$54,717

DISBURSEMENTS:

Direct Missions Program	$ 1,583
Cooperative Program	12,403
Radio and Cablevision Ministry	511
Local Benevolence	189
Christian Service Center	48
Sunday School and Church Training	2,548
Woman's Missionary Union	49
Men of the Church	102
Music Ministry Supplies	359
Boy Scout Program	
Baptist Record	39
Church Library	96
Youth Activities	973
Pastor	2,318
Car Allowance	300
Home and Utility Allowance	458
Minister of Education and Administration	1,576
Car Allowance	150
Home and Utility Allowance	333
Minister of Activities	960
Car Allowance	75
Home and Utility Allowance	413
Music Ministry	1,372
Church Secretary	996
Financial Secretary	561
Educational Secretary	231
Nursery Attendants	319
Nursery Director	134
Janitors	1,887
Maintenance Supervisor	388
Annuity	875
Social Security	589
	182
	2,075
	490
	389
	210
	(41)
	765
	243
	256
	1,310
	8,368
Pulpit Supp.	207
Maintenance	422
Pastor's Conv	23
Staff's Conve	118
Miscellaneous	125
Miscellaneous	81
Baptist Childr	335
Christmas Fun	434
Rand Property	522
Training Progr	20
TOTAL DI	(60)
Cash in Bank —	311
	525
	$50,145
	$17,614

564 Pledges = $1,043,376.66!

The Freedom to Grow Capital Fund Drive was successfully completed on April 28, 1982 — the 125th Birthday of Plymouth Church.

564 gifts or pledges have been made for a total of $1,043,376.66. This fine achievement was made possible by a great number of small and moderate sized gifts ($75,000 was the largest single gift).

A handsome leather bound book including all contributions and pledges was presented to the congregation by the Co-chairpersons of the campaign, Barbara Laederach and Dave Buran, at the birthday celebration in April. The book is on display at the church.

Our congregation can be justly proud of this accomplishment which has allowed the installation of our fine new organ; worship center expansion and a new sound system in the sanctuary; insulation of the sanctuary and other areas of the plant; and installation of thermopane windows in many parts of the building.

A number of deferred or planned gifts have been made and a committee will continue to offer information and aid for those who wish to support Plymouth in this way in the coming years.

Approximately $200,000 is still out in pledges and will be forthcoming through 1984. As this money becomes available the endowment fund of the church will benefit.

Through the enthusiastic and devoted effort of many people and the generous and positive response of a broad base of our congregation we have indeed enhanced our freedom to grow.

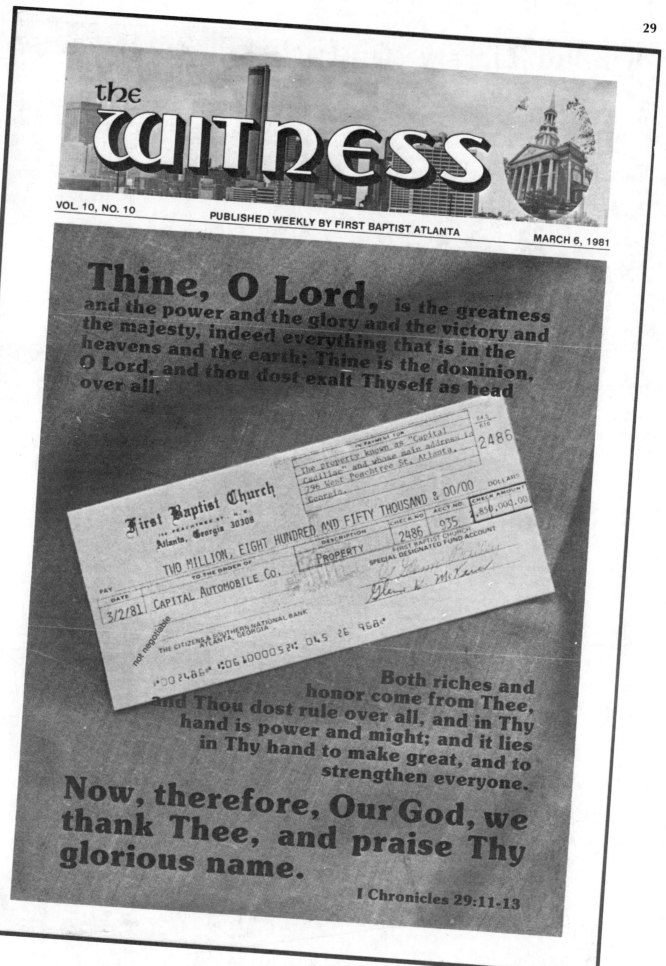

Three Approaches to Stewardship Promotion

Plymouth Library: 'One of the Finest I've Seen'

By Lois Thompson

"Plymouth has one of the finest church libraries I've seen," a patron recently told Joanne Lee, librarian, and a visit quickly reveals that it offers a wide assortment of materials to meet a wide range of interests.

"Special shelves" offer easy access to books on timely topics. The "Free to be ..." shelf has information about sexual stereotyping, how to identify "pigeonholing," and how all persons may attain their greatest potential.

There is a section for drug dependency and alcoholism, and it includes books written for children. There is also a shelf devoted to religious cults.

Photo Album

Two notebooks are of particular interest, one of benevolences and one a photograph album of new members. The notebook of benevolences contains a descriptive brochure of each organization to which Plymouth gives financial support. The other has pictures of new members of Plymouth Church, and will help you connect names to the right faces. Ask the librarian to show you these books.

Works of fiction and biography are popular with many Plymouth readers, and there are art books galore. Teachers, parents, and handwork enthusiasts find the handicraft books-a rich source of ideas for projects to make.

You will also find current books on social issues and family problems, such as divorce, remarriage, the single parent, and aging.

World Religions

The library has an abundance of books about the Bible, theology, Christianity and other world religions. The reference section includes many aids for Bible study — dictionaries, encyclopedias, commentaries and atlases.

check out. Cassette tapes of Sunday worship services are in steady demand, and there are also tapes of sermons from earlier years, featuring Dr. Howard Conn, The Reverend Hugh Jones, and Dr. Howard Thurman.

Young readers enjoy their own corner where they find picture books, popular fiction and nonfiction suited to their individual reading level.

Church Library Awareness Article

BOOK REVIEWS

You and Your Thoughts - The Power of Right Thinking by Earl D. Radmacher. Tyndale, pages, $1.95.

In an age of messed up minds and erratic thinking, *You and Your Thoughts* reads like a fresh breeze. With crisp and concise style Dr. Radmacher outlines some basic concepts that pack a common sense wallop. Right thinking is vital to the believer's spiritual growth and productivity.

I would recommend *You and Your Thoughts* for any Christian, but it is of particular value as a follow up tool for new believers. The battle against Satan's insidious attack on the mind can be waged more effectively with these insights.

—Reviewed by Pastor Bixby

The Minister's Library by Cyril J. Barber. Baker Books, 482 pages, $12.95.

The Minister's Library is an extremely valuable and useful book for the young pastor or seminary student. It will help him to organize and build an orderly, useful library to make him more effective in the ministry.

The first section of the book gives practical helps on classifying and cataloging. It includes a complete alphabetical subject guide to Dewey Decimal Classification. The remainder of the book is a comprehensive bibliography of suggested books for the pastor's library. A brief description of each is included. I highly recommend this aid to pastors of all ages and experiences.

When Can I Say 'I Love You'? by Max and Vivian Rice. Moody Press

When Can I Say 'I Love You' is a very readable book for both youth and for their parents. The authors deal with many common questions teens ask regarding dating, love and marriage. Using a Biblical basis they have given answers which will direct youth to have Godly relationships with the opposite sex. For instance, in answering the question "How do I know it's love?", projects are suggested from I Corinthians 13 and other passages to help one to definitely know. Other questions are handled with special insight and suggested practical projects. The suggested projects are valuable to all who are working with teens. I would highly recommend this book for teens, young adults and parents.

—Reviewed by Pastor Hammond

Book Review Column

MEET THE TEACHERS . . .

JIM AND SUE QUIGGINS

Jim and Susan Quiggins met at Trevecca and were married just after graduating in 1971.

Susan Patton Quiggins, a parsonage daughter from Knoxville, graduated with the BS degree in elementary education and now is in her tenth year of teaching. She presently teaches third grade at the Bell-aire School.

Jim came to Nashville from Louisville, Kentucky. After his Trevecca graduation he earned the MA degree at Illinois State University. The couple then moved to Kansas where Jim did his doctoral work. He received the Ph.D. in communications and human relations from the University of Kansas and Susan taught in elementary schools there.

The Quigginses were First Church people when they were students; so when they returned to Nashville six years ago they came right back to their first love. Dr. Quiggins had returned to head the Communications Department at Trevecca and is now chairman of the Departments of Communications and English.

Among Dr. Quiggins' many other duties is the management of the college radio station, WNAZ. This was not new to him since he had had charge of the station when he was a student. WNAZ carries the live broadcasts of the First Church Sunday services.

Teaching five-year-olds in Sunday School has become a standard part of the Quigginses' service to the church.

"Having a child of our own made us want to give our very best in teaching other children," Mrs. Quiggins said. "The children are so innocent and so full of fresh ideas that they make us look again at ourselves," she added.

Their child is tiny Amy, born in 1978.

Jim and Susan can be counted on for a vocal duet in services when asked. Susan sings in the choir as does Jim when other duties permit. He has also served on the church board.

The couple lives in Antioch.

— Edna McConnell

Focus on
Sunday School Teachers

Sunday School Department of the Month

Department of the Month honors go to the Adult 4 Department for the month of January.

Carl Rayfield is Department Director, Mrs. Marcie Brigham and Art Gentry, teachers, and Wilson Jones, substitute teacher.

Mrs. Garner Neely serves as Department Secretary, and Miss Charline Roby and George Cummings, Jr., are outreach leaders.

Congratulations to Adult 4 which becomes the first Adult department to attain this honor in our Sunday School.

Focus on Sunday School Groups

LIFE AND WORK LESSON THIS SUNDAY

We continue the study on "The Church, Inside and Out". The material centers around gifts that each Christian is given by the Spirit. For the Christian cause to advance, many different tasks must be accomplished. No one person has all of the abilities needed to accomplish these tasks. A variety of abilities are needed and are available through Christian people. The Holy Spirit gives spiritual gifts to all believers. Believers must seek to discover and exercise these gifts, for we shall be held responsible for how we have used our God-given gifts. You will want to join in your class this Sunday for this pertinent discussion.

Sunday School Lesson Preview

RADIO REACHES OUT MINISTERING TO MANY

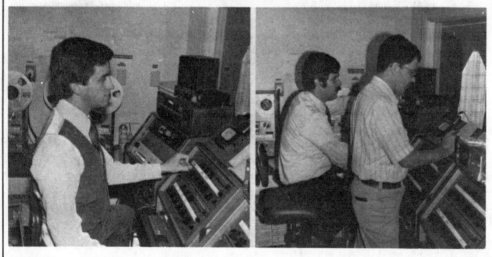

Services of First Church Nashville are broadcast every Sunday (unless technical difficulties intervene). There are many who cannot attend services and enjoy listening to the radio.

The services are broadcast at 8:30 a.m. and 6:30 p.m. on Sunday. Both broadcasts are live. Transmission is over WNAZ, 89.1 FM.

Norman Neeley, pictured above in left photo, has been responsible for the morning radio transmission for the past three and a half years. Norman is now with Federal Aviation, Albuquerque, New Mexico, having taken a new job.

In the right picture is Paul Troutman, standing, who has engineered the 6:30 p.m. service since First Church went on the air about a year ago. Paul works with the Sound Tech Team that provides sound for the sanctuary.

Steve Mays, seated, is active in the church sound system.

If you are a listener to the services on the radio, please let us know. Your response help guide the planning and budgeting of this radio outreach. Our thanks to all those wl make the transmission possible.

This photograph was taken in the sound booth located in the balcony of the main sar tuary of First Church.

Photo Feature on Special Church Ministry

August 10, 1980

In the Church:
For Baptism:
Stephen Banks, Rt. 2, Box 466, 108 Alta, CD4B.

By Letter:
Nancy Dixon, 2205 Beckett C-12, ADS1, from Parkview Baptist Church, Monroe, La.

Janet Vail, 6800 Rasberry Lane, Apt. 2401, Shreveport, ADS2, from Mt. Zion Baptist Church, Coushatta, La.

Introducing
New Church Members

Memo from McEachern

to the following couples who were married on Saturday: **Sherri Jones** and **French Rogers Bolen; Alison Johnson** and **Jeff Peak;**

to **Rick Binder** on receiving the Eagle Scout Award. His Eagle project was to install a drainage system at Central Chapel;

to **Marion** and **Edith Edmonds** who became grandparents of three children in less than a week. Sarah in Asheville has a second daughter, and Marion (Eddie), their son, and his wife in Columbia have twins;

to **Walter Pamplin** on his retirement from Piedmont Natural Gas Company;

to **S. C. & Marjie Ray.** They have been invited by the **Ray Benfields** to serve their church in Salzburg, Austria, September-December, 1983. The Benfields, who are members of our church will be on furlough four months. The Rays will live in their home and pastor the English-speaking church;

to **Cindy Miller** who entered Wake Forest as a freshman for 1982-83;

to **D. B. Cobb, R. Kent Floyd, Mrs. Helen Matthews, Mrs. Mary Jon Roach,** and **Dr. Helen Stinson** who were ordained as deacons on last Sunday.

Fellowship-Building
Pastor's Column

HAPPY BIRTHDAY

FRIDAY, May 1
Mrs. J.L. Blalock, 407 Pinehurst Dr.
Mrs. Donald Burk, 907 Euclid Ave.
Mrs. Loretta G. Coram, 906 Stanton Ave.
Miss Becky McQuaig, 711 Atlantic Ave.
Mr. L.H. Reynolds, 1605 Osceola Ave.
Mrs. Martha Tyre, 504 Fern St.
SATURDAY, May 2
Mrs. M.J. Carswell, 607 Community Dr.
Walter Eugene Godwin, 114 Highland Dr.
Mr. Bill Holt, 626 Owens St.
Jenny McQuaig, 601 Fern St.
SUNDAY, May 3
Mrs. Kate Griffin, 704 Brunel St.
Mrs. Corinne Hammond, 310 Community Dr.
Mr. Herbert Hitson, Rt. 1, Box 81-G
MONDAY, May 4
Mrs. John Beach, 401 Pineview Dr.
Mrs. Pearlie Dorminey, 600 Summit St.,
Apt. C-1
Miss Missy Guinn, 516 Crescent St.
Mr. Lee Pirkle, Rt. 5, Box 501
Shari Strickland, 1604 Darling Ave.
TUESDAY, May 5
Mrs. Bennie Ricketson, 1929 Ben Hill Ave.
Mrs. Vincent Settle, 713 Magnolia Dr.
Mrs. Patti Tanner, Rt. 3, Box 141
WEDNESDAY, May 6
Mrs. Eddie Dryden, 507 Spurgeon St.
THURSDAY, May 7
Mrs. Bessie Berry, 1601 Riverside Dr.
Mrs. M.F. Cowart, 812 Reed St.
Mr. H.E. Dill, 1108 Cherokee Circle
Mr. Euell McClung, 1207 Stanton Ave.
Mr. C.W. Phillips, 1300 Dean Dr.
Mr. Corey Thornton, Blackshear, Ga.
FRIDAY, May 8
Mr. T.W. Booth, 608 Preston St.
Mr. Sam DuBose, 1304 Hill St.
Mr. Jimmy Heath, 527 Kenwood Dr.
Mrs. Joan Murray, Rt. 5, Box 139
SATURDAY, May 9
Mrs. Claire Blanton, 1408 Village Rd. Apt. 1
Drew Dorminey, 1401 Darling Ave.

Happy Birthday Column

BABY OF THE WEEK

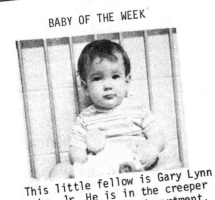

This little fellow is Gary Lynn Vaughn, Jr. He is in the creeper class in the nursery department. His proud daddy is Gary Vaughn.

I want to thank every one at Grace who prayed for us while my son was in the hospital. He is at home and doing fine.
Mrs. T. M. Megar, Sr.

****

I want to thank the staff and my many friends at Grace for the visits, cards, flowers, prayers and love shown to me while I was in the hospital. There is no place like Grace. --Mrs. Ruth Johnson

****

I want to thank Bro. Fred, Bro. Summar and other friends at Grace for their visits, cards, prayers and other kindness shown "Buck" while he was in the hospital. You'll never know just what they meant to both of us. We love you all.
--Mrs. Oca Guthrie

Two Ways to Say "Thank You"

Thank You

. . . .to Helen and Dick Vogel, who have retired as head sacristans, having completed their two-year term very faithfully and competently.

. . . .to The Rev. Erwin Boettcher, Chaplain of Moravian Manor, and friend of our congregation, who so generously made emergency hospital visits to our members while Rev. Peterson was out-of-town.

. . . .from Ted and Adele Grosh, for the prayers, cards, visits and other indications of concern shown them during Ted's recent illness and Adele's incapacitation with a broken wrist.

. . . .from Caryl Langford, for all the kindnesses and Christian love shown her during her hospitalization.

. . . .to Tracy Campbell, for so ably filling our pulpit February 14.

. . . .from the Youth Fellowship to everyone who supported their recent bake sale.

. . . .to Bob Girvin, for his many years as treasurer of the Christian Education Committee.

Baby-of-the-Week Feature

PLYMOUTH PROFILE: Dick and Vivian Stuck

By Jim Noah

Dick and Vivian Stuck in many respects epitomize the growing membership of Plymouth Congregational Church. They "found Plymouth" in the late 1960's after searching for some time for a church which would provide them "a vehicle for involvement with their community."

Native Minnesotans and residents of Minneapolis all their adult lives, Dick and Vivian have supplied creative impetus and organization to the growing social ministry activity of Plymouth Church for the past decade.

Vivian Stuck's desire for community participation has also been reflected in her employment during the past five years with the Dayton Hudson Foundation.

Leadership

At Plymouth Church Vivian's creative-management ability was recognized early in the 1970's through her contributions as a Neighborhood Board Member. Subsequently, she worked for two years as a staff member at Plymouth as Coordinator of Neighborhood Services, providing valuable leadership in the conception and implementation of social programs. She maintains her church activity, at present,

as Chairperson of the Benevolence Committee of the Board of Deacons.

Dick Stuck, of Dick Stuck & Associates (a Minneapolis based advertising agency), has maintained his support of Plymouth Church activities in a less visible but no less dynamic fashion. The unheralded application of his skills as a communicator have contributed to the fruition of a variety of social and educational activities over the past several years. Many members over the congregation recall Dick's leadership in promoting and establishing a seminar for the church fellowship on Native American Education.

Shifting Needs

In talking with Dick and Vivian, one is impressed by their conviction that a church should function as a center of neighborhood activity in a positive and pragmatic way. They are pleased that Plymouth has, over the years, demonstrated an ability to recognize and respond to the shifting needs of the community in which it functions. "Relating to the real world," as Dick puts it, is imperative if a church is going to have a societal impact. Plymouth Congregational Church, believes Dick, has an ability to

"make room for everybody" and function as a viable forum for the discussion and consideration of today's often confusing array of social problems.

Dick and Vivian have two daughters. Susan lives in Paris, France and operates her own catering service. She is married to Jason Newman, an American attorney and consultant to a French law firm. Susan's sister, Mary, is an archaeologist: she and her husband Stuart Lovejoy work for the U.S. Forest Service in northern California.

Vivian and Dick Stuck

The talk of children causes a person to think of the future. As regards the future of Plymouth Church, Vivian and Dick are both hopeful and concerned. They are greatly concerned about the dramatically changing social structure in which we find ourselves living today and very hopeful that Plymouth will generate sufficient community activity to meet the challenge. With people like Vivian and Dick Stuck in its fellowship Plymouth Congregational Church faces its social responsibilities with direction, energy, and innovation.

Feature Article on Outstanding Church Members

SCRIPTURE MEMORY

The following boys and girls were awarded Children's Living Bibles for faithfulness in scripture memory'.

Grade 1: Paul Matthews, Danny Mullis, Chuck Simmons, Michael Miller.

Grade 2: David Taylor, Christi Grisham, Laura Burns, Belinda Yozuiak, Jay Carr.

Grade 3: Katherine Boyd, Rita Bryant, Kelly Clark, Rex Cooper, Troy Farr, Diane Fincher, Jori Hamrick, Jennifer Jordan, Krista McDaniel, Ivey Miller.

Grade 4: Tonya Stuckey, Allison Woodell

Grade 5: Brad Bosworth, Christy Carr, Amy Clark, Kathy Fincher, Chris Watson, Stephanie Taylor, Christie Simmons.

Grade 6: Kevin Ball, James Flanagan, Kenneth Holloway, Bruce Jordan, Todd Killingsworth, Jill Perkins.

Recognition for Accomplishments

Idleknots Busy All Summer

The Idleknots have been living up to their name and certainly have not been idle all summer!

The biggest project of the summer was their participation in the Gilford Old Home Day on August 29.

At their booth they displayed the quilt, rocking chair and lamp that they have been selling tickets on since the Ascension Thursday Banquet. Many people stopped to take chances and to buy the various arts and crafts projects on sale.

The raffle netted $372.00 and the sale earned $360.35. The proceeds have been turned over to the Guild for future projects.

The winners of the raffle were announced at the first Guild meeting. The first prize, a quilt in the Roman stripe pattern, was won by Judy Hook of Gilford, the second prize, a rocking chair donated by Harris Furniture was won by Joyce E. Whitcomb of Laconia and the third prize, a ceramic lamp with cut-and-punch shade made by Ray and Joya Ouellette, went to Mary Ellen Desjardins of Saco, Maine.

The Idleknots are meeting every Thursday from one to four and are planning another quilt. Once again they invite anyone who likes to sew to join them.

Focus on a Special Church Group

SECOND ANNUAL FAITH
INVITATIONAL—NO EXCUSES
NOT FOR MEN ONLY GOLF TOURNEY

SATURDAY, AUGUST 22   8:00 A.M.

WINNEGAMIE GOLF COURSE
NEENAH
18 Holes

Carts Available

$1.00 and Green Fees
Includes Prizes and Refreshments
(Quantity of refreshments depends upon quantity of people)

TRAVELING TROPHIES

Women's Low Score	Men's Low Score
Women's Low Handicap Score	Men's Low Handicap Score

The Order of the Shanked Shot
(Handicap based upon random draw of six holes)

PRIZES

Closest To Pin, Longest Drive *(and whatever else we think up before the 22nd)*

SPECIAL RULES

Each player is allowed one mulligan and one lost ball without penalty (Not transferable)
   (If you do not know what a mulligan is, ask Bill Selle)
   (If you do not know what a lost ball is, this invitation is hereby revoked)

Anyone heard uttering an excuse of any kind after a bad shot is fined 50¢ into the
   refreshment fund. (25¢ if you turn yourself in)

Anyone heard asking the divinity to condemn a golf club, ball, player, the organizers
   of this outing, or anything else to eternal "weeping and gnashing of teeth"
   shall be fined 50¢ to the refreshment fund.
   (Lip reading from across the fairway is enough to turn in someone)

PLAY IS BY RESERVATION ONLY

YOU MUST SIGN UP ON THE NARTHEX POSTER OR CALL ALAN KLAAS (734-1612)

BY WEDNESDAY, AUGUST 19

-9-

Fellowship-Building "Just-for-Fun" Promotion

Bible Verse For The Week

When I was a child, I spake as a child, I understood as a child, I thought as a child: but when I became a man, I put away childish things. For now we see through a glass darkly; but then face to face: now I know in part; but then shall I know even as also I am known. And now abideth faith, hope, charity, these three; but the greatest of these is charity.
I Corinthians 13:11-13

Bible Verse Feature

Thot For The Week:

Mothers write on the hearts of their children what the world's rough hand cannot erase.

Inspiring Thoughts

FALL PREACHING SCHEDULE

10:30 a.m. in the sanctuary

September 12 — Vivian Jones
Rally Day
September 19 — Vivian Jones
September 26 — Meditation by
Vivian Jones
Vignettes from "A Balancing Act"
October 3 — Meditation by
Vivian Jones
World Wide Communion Sunday
October 10 — Vivian Jones
October 17 — Vivian Jones
October 24 — Cyril Davey
October 31 "Casa Materna"
— Vivian Jones
"A Church for God"
November 7 — Vivian Jones
"A Church for Others"
November 14 — Vivian Jones
"A Church for Us" —
Stewardship Sunday
November 21 — Vivian Jones
November 28 — Meditation by
Gary Reierson
Advent Communion
December 5 — Elaine Marsh
Advent II
December 12 — Vivian Jones
Advent III
December 19 — Vivian Jones
Advent IV
December 26 — Gary Reierson

Preaching Schedule Promotion

A SERMON BY DR. McCLUSKEY THAT WONDROUS CROSS

The subject today comes from the words of Sir Isaac Watts hymn, "When I Survey the Wondrous Cross." I love the words of this hymn. Sir Isaac Watts wanted to be remembered as a pastor of a London church, but he is remembered as a great hymn writer. He lived from 1678 until 1748 and in 1703 he published this hymn. He is the author of more than 100 hymns. It is interesting that 17 of these are found in the current Baptist Hymnal. You are familiar with many of them: "At the Cross", "Jesus Shall Reign Where'er the Sun", "Joy to the World", "O God, Our Help in Ages Past", "We're Marching to Zion", "When I Can Read My Title Clear", "Am I A Soldier of the Cross." But the hymn we are focusing our attention on today, "When I Survey the Wondrous Cross", has been called the greatest Christian hymn ever written.

We are going to sing one stanza of this hymn at each of the main points of the message. Please open your hymnal to No. 111 and keep your hymnal in one hand and your Bible in the other. Let us sing the first stanza of "When I Survey the Wondrous Cross."

When I survey the wondrous cross,
On which the Prince of glory died,
My richest gain I count but loss,
And pour contempt on all my pride.

When I survey the wondrous cross I see a great savior. Those of the first century would have been amazed to have heard the cross called "a wondrous cross." The cross was a symbol of suffering and shame. A popular saying was, "cursed is he who dies upon a cross." The cross was a means of capital punishment. It was a cruel way to put evil men to death. It had far more stigma than a hangman's gallows, the electric chair, or the gas chamber would have today. How then can we call it a wondrous cross] Jesus died on a cross. For that reason we can call it a wondrous cross. I want you to look at the cross and think about the person who died there. Sometimes we see a crucifix, a cross with an image or a picture of Jesus on it. We are sometimes critical of those who use a crucifix. We say that Jesus should not be shown on the cross. Rather we should remember the cross is empty and that Christ is alive! There is a certain truth in that, and yet sometimes we forget that it is because of Jesus that the cross can be called a glorious cross. The steeples of churches are decorated with the cross and stained glass windows contain its image. We wear pieces of jewelry in the form of the cross. In many ways we have made something of beauty of the cross. But I would remind you that it was an old, rugged cross upon which Jesus died-- "an emblem of suffering and shame!" Any time we look at the cross, we need to remember that we do not worship the cross, but instead we worship the Christ.

During the time of Oliver Cromwell in England, there was a war. The vicar of a famous church was afraid the enemy was going to capture the church. In the church hung a beautiful silver cross. He asked permission to remove the cross and put it into hiding for safe-keeping. Reluctantly, Oliver Cromwell finally agreed. But only with the understanding there would be engraved on the back side of that silver cross these words, "We worship the Christ, not the cross." When we behold the cross, let us remember that the Prince of glory died there and that it is because of Jesus Christ that the cross is a *wondrous* cross.

When I survey the wondrous cross I see a great sacrifice. Let us sing the second stanza of this hymn.

Forbid it Lord, that I should boast,
Save in the death of Christ my God;
All the vain things that charm me most,
I sacrifice them to his blood.

Open your Bibles to I Peter 1:18-19 as we think about the greatness of the sacrifice on the cross. Peter writes, "Forasmuch as ye know that ye were not redeemed with corruptible things,

Con't on pg. 2

Sermon Excerpt

Family Focus:
Don't Let Depression Get You Down!

By LESLIE THOMPSON

After the flurry of the Christmas holidays has subsided, and everyone has rested up from the sore backs and pulled muscles of snow-shoveling, the 'February Lull' begins. All the talk shows on television and all the magazines' need to focus on a new issue. This year it's "depression".

"20-20" recently presented a Depression Test to viewers - if you answered "yes" to enough questions, you were depressed enough to seek professional help. But everyone gets depressed sometimes; where can you draw the line between "normal" and "serious" episodes of depression.

According to "Current Medical Diagnosis and Treatment", a physician's reference book, the whole issue of depression is confused because the word itself is used so many ways - a mood, a sympton, a syndrome, or a disease. Depression is a reality of everyday life, and can be a normal reaction to a great variety of events. Not every depression requires treatment.

The symptoms present in most cases were listed: lowered mood, from mild sadness to intense guilt and hopelessness; difficulty in concentrating and inability to make decisions; loss of interest, with diminished involvement in work and recreation; complaints such as headache, disrupted, lessened or excessive sleep; decreased sexual drive; anxiety.

Perhaps a physician could make the issue simpler. I called Dr. Terrence Murphy, a Brookline internist affiliated with St. Elizabeth's Hospital.

"What is depression, Dr. Murphy?"

"Everyone gets down and blue feeling at times." Dr. Murphy answered. "It's normal when it's the response to appropriate stimuli, like a death in the family or a disappointment.

"I worry when the patient can't recover from the event - when the depression is so severe that it interfers with the ability to function for a long time. By this I mean eating, sleeping, usual activity. And certainly it is serious if there are thoughts of taking one's life."

Dr. Murphy explained that there are two types of depression: "exogenous", caused by external stimuli, and "endogenous", occurring for no apparent reason. If there is a family history of depression, there may be an endogenous cause - a chemical imbalance that can be corrected with medication.

"A patient who seems to be on an emotional roller coaster - with very dramatic swings from periods of over-activity, euphoria and then deep depression for no apparent reason - should see their regular doctor or internist to make a determination. There are good, effective drugs available, when indicated," advised Dr. Murphy.

"Depression can also mask as unrelated minor physical complaints, excessive absentee-ism from work or school, sleep problems, or excessive drug or alcohol use.

"Loss is the most common cause of 'normal' depression, and acknowledgement takes time. Going through the rituals of wake and funeral is a very important part of the process. Get back to normal routine as soon as possible." The amount of time one should expect this normal depression to last is 2 weeks, and then improvement should begin.

So don't let depression or quizes get you down! Help and medication are available when needed. Call your doctor if:

1. you are thinking of suicide or there is a family history of depression.

2. you are depressed deeply or for a prolonged period of time for no apparent reason.

3. you are experiencing cycles of dramatic emotional swing from euphoria to depression.

4. you cannot recover from a normal depression after a reasonable period of time.

And remember some of the best listeners anywhere are waiting to be supportive at our own rectory.

Counseling Column

HOLINESS AND HOLLYWOOD

Hollywood, California advertises itself as "The Entertainment Capital of the World." It is the headquarters of the moving pictures industry. Next to television, no medium of entertainment exerts a stronger influence on more people than the movies. The potential for good is unlimited.

Unfortunately, holiness and Hollywood are as far apart as the poles! Abundant evidence of this fact is contained in the theater advertisements in the newspapers.

By its own rating system, hardly one movie in a hundred is judged by the movie industry to be fit for family viewing.

In light of the frightening moral damage done by Hollywood movies, our Christian responsibility includes the obligation to witness against social evils and by the refusal to patronize an industry known to be purveyous of pornography and violence.

Many religious, educational and wholesome programs are available through the television medium but they are far from having a competitive portion of the industry.

Parents must carefully monitor the programs which are watched by their children and confine their viewing to that which contributes to their mental, emotional and spiritual enrichment.

NOW is the time for God's people everywhere to take an uncompromising stand against an industry which makes available such morally degrading filmfare which tends to destroy the most sacred units of society-the home.

Anything less is unworthy of our holy calling.

submitted by Lay Leader,

Melvin McBee

Opinion Article on a Social Issue

BIBLE JUMBLES

Old Testament	New Testament
veil is cut ___	cats ___
see sing ___	what met ___
mapsls ___	one tar veil ___
sob revrp ___	sew herb ___
and lie ___	kram ___
ton meat nails ___	nails a tag ___
sox due ___	sittu ___
o nero my duet ___	pane is she ___
rich conels ___	lemon hip ___
cic sees slate ___	is no thin car ___

OLD TESTAMENT BOOKS: Leviticus, Genesis, Psalms, Proverbs, Daniel, Lamentations, Exodus, Deuteronomy, Chronicles, Ecclesiastes

NEW TESTAMENT BOOKS: Acts, Matthew, Revelation, Hebrews, Mark, Galatians, Titus, Ephesians, Philemon, Corinthians

CHILDREN'S CORNER

ANNOUNCING! AN ART CONTEST!

For all those under the age of 15.
Rules: (1) The picture must portray one of the miracles of Jesus. (2) No larger than 5½ x 8½" (½ sheet of reg. paper) (3) Deadline: May 23--winners announced June 13. (4) All entries must have name and age of artist and title of picture. (5) Three best entries will be printed in the newsletter. (6) All entries will be displayed at the church. (7) The 1st place winner will receive an award of $15, second place $8, and third place $5. (8) No more than 3 entries per person. (9) Each person entering will receive a special prize.

CHILDREN'S LETTERS TO GOD

Dear Jesus, I am thankful for a home, food, and education. I am thankful for friends, clothing, and a family. I am thankful for to live and to be free. I am also thankful for mother nature, the animals in the forest, and to be happy.
Love, Michael"

"Dear Jesus Thank you for our food clothes and shoes. Thank you for my dog my brothers and sisters and parents and aunts and uncles thank you for being helthey thank you for a mother making mony in work & a father who is working and so we can go get good from Demoulers and thank you for haveing friends and thank you for going to florida and havening a birthday Amen.
love Lisa Ann H. !!!!"

Three Special Features for Children

COOKING CORNER

STRAWBERRY SHORTCUT CAKE

1 cup minature marshmallows
2 cups sliced strawberries "frozen in syrup and thawed"
1 pkg. (3 oz.) strawberry gelatin
2½ cups flour
1½ cup sugar
½ cup shortening
3 tsp. baking powder
½ tsp. salt
1 cup milk
1 tsp. vanilla
3 eggs

Grease a 9 x 13 pan. Sprinkle the marshmallows evenly over bottom of pan and set aside. Thoroughly combine the strawberries along with their syrup and gelatin and set aside. In a large bowl, combine flour, sugar, shortening, baking powder, salt, milk, vanilla and eggs. Blend at low speed until moistened. Beat 3 minutes at medium speed. Pour over marshmallows. Spoon strawberry mixture over the batter and bake for 45 to 50 minutes at 350 degrees.

Recipe Feature

GENERAL CHURCH NEWS IN BRIEF
From Nazarene News Service
Melodye Jones, Editor

NEW GENERAL BOARD MEMBER ELECTED—Rev. Gilbert M. Hughes, pastor of the Muncie, Ind., Southside Church of the Nazarene this week was elected to serve as a General Board Member representing the Central U.S.A. Region. Rev. Hughes' election fills a vacancy on the General Board created when Rev. Gerald Green of Seymour, Ind., passed away earlier this year. Ordained in 1951 by the Northwest Indiana District, Rev. Hughes is a graduate of Olivet Nazarene College and Nazarene Theological Seminary. He served five pastorates on the Illinois District from 1954-1981 when he moved to the Muncie church. Rev. Hughes and his wife, Naydine have one son, Darrell Hughes.

MID-AMERICA NAZARENE COLLEGE HAS ANNOUNCED THAT THE MABEE FOUNDATION of Tulsa, Okla., has awarded a challenge grant to the college in the amount of $750,000. These funds will be used for the "Cornerstone and Wiscom Campaign" which includes a new library building, renovation of the present library for use as an administration building and classroom facilities, and renovation of the Osborn building for use as a science facility.

Column of Denominational News

WMU MISSION ACTION SURVEY

NAME _____ SUNDAY SCHOOL CLASS _____

ADDRESS _____

TELEPHONE NO. (Home) _____ (Business) _____

Education: (Please circle)

Grade 6 7 8 9 10 11 12 High School Graduate □
Vocational Training □   College 1 2 3 4
Degree earned: _____ Major: _____

Interests:

—In which age group do you prefer to work: □ Preschool □ Children □ Youth □ Adults □ Senior Adults

—What type of experience have you had? Sunday School, Church Training, Missions, Music (Circle One) _____Other

Have you had experience in:

□ Art
□ Advertising
□ Interior Decorating
□ Typing
□ Bookkeeping
□ Office Machines
□ Food Service
□ Nursing Care
□ First Aid
□ Counseling
□ Mission Trips
□ Youth Retreats
□ Story Telling
□ Financial Planning
□ House Painting
□ Teaching Music
□ Dental or Medical
□ Play Musical Instrument

□ Baby Sitting
□ Teaching Languages
□ Library Science
□ Media Services
□ Literacy Classes
□ Tutoring
□ Bus Driver
□ Floral Arrangements
□ Carpentry
□ Painting
□ Wall Papering
□ Plumbing
□ Sewing
□ Others:_____

I Would Be Willing To Help Through:

1. Transportation: Local □ Atlanta □
2. Clothing: Age_____ Sex_____ Size_____
3. Food □
4. Financial (No Cash): Utilities □ Clothing □ Gasoline □ Medical □ Glasses □ Housing □
5. Housing: Temporary □ Permanent □ Furnished □ Unfurnished □
6. Employment: Full Time □ Part Time □ Skills required_____
7. Other: _____

Gathering Information Through the Newsletter

4
How to Put Visual Appeal into Your Church Paper

Visual appeal refers to a newsletter's graphic design and its impact on the reader. Good eye appeal in printed materials of all types is essential these days because of the influence of television and other visual forms of communication. Many people today have become lazy readers; they won't bother to read anything unless it's presented in an interesting, attractive package.

How do you put this magic ingredient called *visual appeal* into each issue of your newsletter? How do you shape it into a package that is attractive, appealing, and interesting to read? This is a quality that eludes many publications, even those with unlimited money to spend. And most church newsletters don't have such luxuries as a full-time staff artist and an offset press that prints in four colors.

But the good news is that certain principles of graphic design apply to any publication, no matter how limited your budget or how antiquated your printing equipment. These foundational principles, if followed consistently, should help you publish a church paper with first-class visual appeal.

Start with a Good First Impression

You have probably heard the old saying, "You never get a second chance to make a good first impression." That's certainly true of a publication. Your readers automatically form opinions about your newsletter the minute they pick it up and scan the front page. Does it come across as interesting or dry, appealing or dull, professional or amateurish? A favorable first impression will encourage readers to turn inside to see what else your publication has to offer.

The first step to a good first impression is a strong, appropriate name for your newsletter. A unique name such as *Trinity Trumpet* is far superior to a generic, general title like "the Trinity newsletter." A specific name gives the newsletter an authentic identity. It also comes across as more professional, helping establish a more favorable image in the minds of your readers. If your church paper doesn't have a specific name, sponsor a "name the newsletter" contest among the membership (see illustration, p. 47). Many churches have found just the right names for their newsletter with this approach.

The second step to a favorable first impression is a crisp

concise design for your newsletter masthead. The masthead is the logo or title of your newsletter, along with the name of your church, that appears at the top of the front page. As an official identification badge, this masthead will be seen over and over again by readers during the course of the church year.

Because of this wide exposure and the image which it projects for your church, the masthead deserves professional treatment. Perhaps there is a commercial artist in your church who would be glad to do such a design at no charge. Or you might hire a local artist or printer for the job. This is one of those cases where it will probably cost to go first class. But the investment will be repaid several times over in terms of professional results.

Even if you reproduce by mimeograph, a customized newsletter design is still a possibility. Have the artist design the masthead to fit your stencil format. Then get a supply of stencils die-impressed with the newsletter masthead design at the top. The front page of each issue of your newsletter can be typed under the masthead right on the stencil. Ask your stencil supplier about this customized die-impressing process. If he doesn't provide the service, he can probably refer you to a firm that does.

OK, so you're convinced your newsletter needs a masthead with a professional design. What makes a masthead outstanding? What elements should the logo for your church paper include? Take a close look at the excellent mastheads from three church newsletters (see illustrations, p. 47). These might serve as models for your own masthead design.

First, notice the large type that's used to display the titles of these three newsletters—*Nazarene Weekly*, *The Flame*, and *Midweek Messenger*. Put the title of your newsletter in bold type like this, with the name of your church in much smaller type. The bold type helps to establish an identity and a strong image for the newsletter and the church in the minds of your readers.

Simple artwork that carries out the theme of your church or the title of the newsletter is also appropriate for the masthead. Notice the flame included in the masthead of the church paper by that title and the simple line drawing of the church in the *Midweek Messenger*. These tasteful illustrations give the mastheads a certain dramatic flair, but they are not so strong that they overwhelm the bold, dark titles of the church papers.

Another characteristic of these masthead designs is compactness. Their crisp, streamlined design leaves plenty of room for a good feature or news article on page 1. As a general rule, the masthead should take up no more than one fourth to one third of the space on the front page.

Standard information that should always be included as a part of your newsletter design includes the name, street address, and city where your church is located and the specific date of that issue of the newsletter. Other helpful information that could be published in this prominent location includes the telephone number, the minister, and the official slogan or motto of the church.

Because of its lead position on the front page, the masthead can be used for some subtle but effective promotion (see illustration, p. 48). This church designed its newsletter title in such a way that small illustrations or blocks of copy can be published on both sides of the masthead. Important events or seasonal themes on the church's schedule are inserted in these spaces for high-visibility promotion.

One good thing about putting your best foot forward is that it often sets the pace for the rest of the trip. If you go to all the trouble of designing a good masthead for your newsletter, why not let it serve as the unifying idea for the whole church paper? This principle was used effectively by one creative church (see illustration, p. 48). The distinctive type in the masthead was also used for the titles of regular features scattered throughout the newsletter. This is a good technique that ties the entire issue together into one harmonious and eye-pleasing package.

Make Sure the Copy Is Easy to Read

Another secret of good visual appeal is readability. Simply stated, this principle means: *Make sure the copy in your church paper is easy to read.* This truth is so obvious that you may wonder about the need to emphasize it. But it's violated so often in church publications that it deserves a thorough examination.

Four common readability problems in church newsletters are illustrated on pages 49-50. Take a careful look at each of these shortcomings as we discuss them here. Illustrating and analyzing these problems should help you avoid them in your own church paper.

One mistake that many newsletter editors make is typing or typesetting the copy too wide for easy reading. This block of copy from one church paper stretches 8″ wide all the way across an 8½x11″ sheet of paper! Your eye has a hard time finding its way from the end of one line back to the beginning of the next. For the maximum in reading ease, a line of copy should not go beyond 40 to 45 characters in length. Notice this sample runs to about 80 characters wide—much too long for easy reading. This readability problem can be solved by breaking the copy into two shorter columns.

Another practice guaranteed to give your readers eye strain is typing a large block of copy in all capital letters. The sample from the front page of one church paper actually repels the eye. It's almost as if the capital letters have joined forces in their uniformity to set up an invisible wall that the human eye can't penetrate. Reading is an exercise in recognition—scanning the irregular shapes of letters to decide what words they form. Capital letters look too much alike, so the reader is unable to scan them quickly and process them into recognizable words and phrases.

This same principle also applies to italics type. The human eye is not accustomed to processing all the swirls and frills that give italics type its unique design. So it naturally rebels at doing all this work when presented with a large block of copy in italics.

To avoid this problem in your newsletter, remember that capital letters and italics should always be used in little doses for variety and contrast—never for large blocks of copy that are designed for quick and easy reading. Even the most loyal church members probably aren't noted for their reading perseverance. Copy that is hard to read probably won't be.

Another common readability problem in church papers is crowding large blocks of copy together without any eye breaks. "The Church Mouse" column (see illustration, p. 50) demonstrates this shortcoming precisely. These short, personal items about church members and church events were run together without paragraph breaks in a column that stretched 6″ deep! Each of these items could have been broken into a separate paragraph for easier reading, like they were by another church in its similar feature, "Keeping Up with Our Fellowship." See how much better the second column comes across? It pulls your eye in and invites you to stay a while.

These four readability shortcomings don't cover all the pitfalls. But they should introduce you to the subject and show you some common problems to avoid. Make sure the copy is easy to read, and you are on the road to a church paper with good visual appeal.

Use Headlines for Variety and Contrast

No one wants to look at a page that contains one big mass of gray copy. To produce a church paper with good visual appeal, you have to break the copy up into small units. And each of these separate features and articles in the publication should be given its own individual headline or title. Headlines serve the very useful purpose of identifying these separate articles. They also break up the page and make it more visually appealing.

Even if you print your church paper by mimeograph, headlines can still add a lot of eye appeal. After you type your headlines, underline them to make them stand out from the rest of the page (see illustration, p. 51). Notice that this newsletter also uses the technique of insetting the headlines in the body of the typewritten copy along the lefthand side of the page. This technique puts some contrast into the page and breaks the mass of gray copy into smaller units.

If you publish your church paper by offset, electronic stencil, or copying machine, you can put a lot more variety into your headlines. Use rub-down transfer type to set headlines in large, bold print that contrasts nicely with the rest of the page. If the text type for your newsletter consists of typewritten copy, your headline type should be 18 to 24 points in size. A 24-point letter is about twice as tall as a typewritten character.

Why go to all the trouble of planning headlines for your newsletter unless you plan to write them in good form? One poorly written headline can spoil the visual balance of an entire page. Let's review some principles of good headline writing by looking at several examples from typical church newsletters (see illustrations, p. 52).

First, look over the column of good headlines on the left. Notice that each of these makes a complete statement; it summarizes what the article is about. This is always a better approach than simply *labeling* the article with a general phrase, such as "Brazil Mission Trip" does in the column on the right. This is an example of a *label* headline. It identifies an article without giving any specifics on what the article is about. Good headlines do more than attract attention; they give important information about the subject under discussion.

Another important truth about the headlines on the left is that each contains a strong verb: "Young Adults *to Visit*," "Baptist Women *Elect*," "Religious Books *Needed*," "VBS *Sets*," and "Pastor *Continues*." You can almost see these actions taking place as you read the headlines. For headlines that really get attention, include strong verbs like these that tell the reader what is happening.

Finally, the headlines on the left are visually appealing because they take up most of the space which they are allotted to fill. This is not true of some of the headlines on the right. Notice the gaps in these examples because the headlines don't fill out the lines. As a general rule, a headline should fill at least two thirds of the column from left to right.

The most unsightly headline in the group is the one that reads "Church Parking Lot Closed to High School Drivers." The word "Church" is left dangling in the middle of the column with oceans of white space on either side. This one word alone takes up only about one fourth of the space in the line. To improve this headline, the editor could have dropped the word "Church," and squeezed the headline into these two lines that would have been almost equal in length:

Parking Lot Closed
To High School Drivers

While we're on the subject, here's another good tip about headlines: Never leave prepositions dangling at the ends of lines. Notice how this rule is violated by the headline that reads, "Council to Plan For/ Year Ahead." It would have been much better with the preposition, "For," moved to the beginning of the next line:

Council To Plan
For Year Ahead

See how much better this headline reads when the preposition and its object are linked directly on the same line? The same principle also applies to conjunctions. Never separate conjunctions like "and" or "but" from the words they link by printing the conjunctions at the ends of lines. Here's an example of the violation of this principle:

Grace Church Anniversary and
Revival To Begin Sunday

To eliminate this problem, the headline could be rewritten like this:

Anniversary, Revival Begin
Sunday at Grace Church

Good headline composition is an exercise in polishing and rewriting, as in the examples above—dropping and adding words until you have a combination that summarizes the article and fills the available space. It's not easy, but it can be fun! And pickiness about headlines can pay off in added visual appeal for your newsletter.

Include Visual Elements to Create Interest

Nothing does more for the visual appeal of your newsletter than artwork and illustrations. Readers are attracted by photographs, drawings, and other visual elements that break up the page and make it more attractive.

One of the best things you can do for your newsletter is to subscribe to a service that provides stencil and clip art especially for church newsletters. Most major denominations provide services like this for their respective churches. Check with your book store or denominational supplier for further information. In addition, you might supplement this material by ordering appropriate artwork from independent suppliers. Several companies that provide clip art and stencil art for churches are listed on page 105 in the resources section of this book.

In addition to buying commercial art, you may be able to do some rough drawings on your own that would add some visual appeal to your newsletter. Artwork doesn't have to be fancy in order to be effective, as the examples from two church newsletters demonstrate (see illustrations, p. 53). The outline drawing of Jesus on the cross was made with a stylus on a stencil. Then the poem was typed on the stencil right over the drawing. It's a simple sketch, but it combines with the printed text to deliver a dramatic impact. The illustration of a group of people in the second example is also a simple piece of art. But it does the job of getting the church members' attention and informing them of a church-wide fellowship.

While we're on the subject of artwork and illustrations, let's nail down a few principles on how to use it effectively.

The most important rule of all is to be temperate in your use of art. Remember that artwork is made to supplement and dress up the copy in your newsletter. It just doesn't work the other way around. If you use too much artwork, it gives your newsletter a carnival image. Look at the two different pages from church newsletters that illustrate this principle (see illustrations, pp. 54-55). The page with three pieces of art comes across as tasteful and pleasing. But the page with six or seven illustrations has a "too busy" image. All these pieces of artwork compete for your attention. The eye flits from one to the other, trying to decide which article to read. Too much artwork can be just as bad as no illustrations at all.

Be careful also about how you group artwork and copy together. One mistake that many church paper editors make is splitting a block of copy right down the middle with an illustration. This layout requires the reader to jump over the illustration to pick up the line that's continued on the right side of the art (see illustration, p. 56). The human eye is not accustomed to bridging gaps like this in reading material, so it rebels against the task. It's much better to move the art over to the left and publish the copy next to the illustration in one unbroken column.

Illustrations are excellent if used tastefully, but they aren't the only visual elements that can put eye appeal into your newsletter. You can also achieve good results with small borders and boxes (see illustrations, p. 56). Decorative frames of this type are ideal tools for dressing up a page. They also help to draw your readers' eyes to important events or concerns that deserve major promotion. But again, use this visual technique sparingly. If you put a box around every item in your newsletter, nothing will be highlighted for special attention.

Arrange Each Page into a Harmonious Unit

All the above principles about visual appeal really come to fruition in your newsletter when you start putting everything together page by page. It does little good to fuss over first impressions, readability, headlines, and artwork unless you're willing to go to the trouble of fitting all these diverse elements together into harmonious page units. What are some guidelines that can help you at this stage of the newsletter production process?

The first principle to remember is to give your pages the right amount of "breathing space." Some newsletter pages have too much copy, while others don't have enough (see illustrations, pp. 57-59). To look visually appealing, a page needs the right balance between copy and white space.

The page with too much copy doesn't have enough space around the headlines. See how they are jammed against the rules and the surrounding copy? A little more white space at these points would have given this page more visual impact and made it easier to read.

Now look at the page that doesn't have enough copy. All the copy was double spaced with triple spacing between the paragraphs. Notice the rivers of white space around the illustration in the lower right corner of the page. Obviously, the editor didn't have enough copy to fill this page, so he

"stretched" it by using this wide spacing technique. The result is a page with zero visual impact. It's so thin that your eyes keep getting lost in all the gaps around the copy. What this page really needed was another article to help fill the space.

Finally, let's examine the page that has just the right balance between copy and white space. Notice how much "breathing space" was left on all sides of the large-type headlines. Large type like this needs a lot more "elbow room" than small text type. And look at the ample margins inside the two boxes on the page. This allows the boxes and the copy inside to do their job of attracting the reader's eye. The entire page is an excellent study in the tasteful use of white space.

Another basic principle of harmonious layout is to place the strongest visual elements at different spots on the page. The example from one newsletter (see illustration, pp. 60-61) shows how this principle works. The three strongest visual elements on this page were the two boxes and the photograph, because they naturally attract the reader's eye. But the newsletter editor made the mistake of placing all three of these elements very close together. Notice how much better the total package comes across when the two boxes are moved to different locations on the page? A little change—but what a big improvement in eye appeal!

The toughest layout problem in the newsletter for most editors is the "catch-all page"—the place where you publish all the little miscellaneous items that don't seem to fit anywhere else. This page usually carries such items as the schedule of activities, welcome to new members, report on attendance and offerings, expressions of sympathy, and a listing of church members in the hospital.

Most of these items are short. Because of space problems, they must be published in streamline fashion with small headings and tiny pieces of art. How can you arrange this miscellaneous assortment into a page design that looks at least a little more exciting than the yellow pages of the telephone directory?

Look at the approaches to this problem used by two different church papers (see illustrations, p. 62). One newsletter prints some of the information in bold type. See how the bold-print items were scattered over the page to add some contrast and visual excitement? The second newsletter enclosed the entire page in a box. Each individual feature on the page was also boxed to separate it clearly from all other items. This technique has the effect of making the whole page hang together as a unit, while categorizing the information for quick assimilation by its readers at the same time.

Learning to think in page units—it's one of the keys to putting together a newsletter with good eye appeal. These basic principles should make you more page-conscious as you put together each issue of your church paper.

Mix Ink and Paper Tastefully

No discussion of eye appeal for the church paper would be

complete without a consideration of ink and paper. Every possible combination of colors of ink and paper has probably been used across the years by church newsletters—red ink on yellow paper, black on blue, gray on gold, purple on buff, red on green, even orange on mustard! Some churches publish a different color combination every issue, thinking this will give the newsletter a certain magic appeal.

But the truth is that this approach doesn't work. If anything, these garish color combinations actually work against the newsletter. How can readers learn to recognize the church paper quickly and easily when it always arrives with the rest of their mail in a different colored dress? A better approach is to decide on one tasteful and appealing color combination and to stick with it consistently for several years. This way, the newsletter can build up some familiarity in the minds of your readers.

If one consistent approach is best, how do you decide on the right combination of colors for ink and paper? The most basic rule is known as the *dark on light* principle. Always use a deep, dark ink on a light, pastel-colored paper. This combination establishes a contrast that makes the page pleasing to the eye and easy to read. Never print your newsletter on a dark-colored paper stock (see illustration, p. 62).

See how difficult it is to read these words against the dark background? And the mood the paper establishes is not exactly light and friendly.

Here are some of the most pleasing and readable ink-and-paper color combinations. Commercial artists and printers have used these combinations for years with favorable results. You might consider some of these for your own church paper.

- Dark blue ink on light blue, light gray, or pale yellow paper.
- Dark brown ink on buff, ivory, pale yellow, or pastel green paper.
- Dark green ink on buff, ivory, or light brown paper.

If all else fails, try good old black ink on plain white paper. This combination is hard to beat for readability.

Eye appeal is one of those magic ingredients that make a big difference in publications. There's no better time than now to start working for this quality in your own newsletter. Meanwhile, let's get down to some specifics about preparing stencils and paste-ups for printing. This subject is explored in the next chapter.

Name Our Newsletter GET YOUR THINKING CAP ON! Our newsletter needs a name. It should be (1) not more than two or three words in length (2) convey a message and (3) be easy to say and remember. Submit as many suggestions as you like by April 1.(drop in offering plate or mail to the church). If two or more people submit the same name the first one received will be the one considered. The winner will receive the New King James Version of the New Testament!

"Name-the-Newsletter" Contest

THE *Nazarene Weekly*

FIRST CHURCH OF THE NAZARENE ● 510 WOODLAND ST. ● NASHVILLE, TENN.

VOLUME 52 AUGUST 22, 1982 NUMBER 34

the **FLame**

PLYMOUTH CONGREGATIONAL CHURCH

JULY 11 - AUGUST 7, 1982
871-7400

MIDWEEK MESSENGER

BRENTWOOD BAPTIST CHURCH · William G. Wilson, Pastor

VOL. 12 DECEMBER 2, 1981 NO. 48

Three Well-Designed Newsletter Mastheads

Subtle Promotion on Both Sides of the Masthead

Unifying the Newsletter Around Masthead Design

April 28, 1981

My Dear People,

This coming weekend promises to be a great one for the Woodstock church. On Saturday night
we will have our Fellowship Dinner together at 6:00 p.m., and then on Sunday morning we will
have a baby dedication service, and I'll be preaching on the exciting theme, "The Evidences
of a Spirit-filled Life". On Sunday evening, we will be blessed by having Sandi Patti Helve-
ring with us in a special Musical Concert. Without question Sandi is one of America's great
young singers. Most of you know that she is Ron and Carolyn Patti's daughter and Sandi is
uniquely gifted in music. Mark this down as a priority evening for you and your family.
Sometime during Sunday evening we will also take time out of the concert to have a baptismal service. We have a number of candidates who want to be baptized, and this is always a
beautiful service.

I need to talk to you briefly about our general offerings. Our weekly operating budget calls
for $3,793 weekly and as of last Sunday (17 weeks) we have received a total amount of
$61,532, which is $2,949 short of reaching budget. I call this to your attention now so all
of us can work together to erase this deficit before the summer months. I would like to
challenge our Body to accept the date of May 31 as "Catch-up Sunday". This will give all
of us an opportunity to bring our operating budget up to its proper level. I know you'll
want to work with us in keeping this aspect of our church strong and healthy. I'll be
talking to you about this a little more later on.

I'm really pleased with the consistent averages we are maintaining in all of our services
this year. During 1981 we have averaged 455 in morning worship, 337 in Sunday School, and
273 in Sunday evening service, and approximately 200 or more on Wednesday evenings. This
is fantastic, and we need to keep doing our best to improve all of these averages as we
move on into 1981.

I appreciated being away for two days for some much needed R & R over the weekend and I
want to thank Sharron Weiss, Bill Swagerty and Jeannette Flynn for preaching for me and,
of course, to Steve Fouts for leading the worship services. Don't we have a great staff?

I'm looking forward to gathering with you for the great Fellowship Dinner that our planning
committee has prepared. I'm sure you will enjoy the exciting program that they have planned.

1. Lines Too Long

EVANGELISM IS ....

TO EVANGELIZE IS TO SPREAD THE GOOD NEWS THAT JESUS CHRIST DIED FOR OUR SINS
AND WAS RAISED FROM THE DEAD ACCORDING TO THE SCRIPTURES, AND THAT AS THE
REIGNING LORD HE NOW OFFERS THE FORGIVENESS OF SINS AND THE LIBERATING GIFT
OF THE SPIRIT TO ALL WHO REPENT AND BELIEVE.   OUR CHRISTIAN PRESENCE IN THE
WORLD IS INDISPENSIBLE TO EVANGELISM, AND SO IS THAT KIND OF DIALOGUE WHOSE
PURPOSE IS TO LISTEN SENSITIVELY IN ORDER TO UNDERSTAND. BUT EVANGELISM IT-
SELF IS THE PROCLAMATION OF THE HISTORICAL, BIBLICAL CHRIST AS SAVIOR AND
LORD, WITH A VIEW TO PERSUADING PEOPLE TO COME TO HIM PERSONALLY AND SO BE
RECONCILED TO GOD.   IN ISSUING THE GOSPEL INVITATION WE HAVE NO LIBERTY TO
CONCEAL THE COST OF DISCIPLESHIP.   JESUS STILL CALLS ALL WHO WOULD FOLLOW
HIM TO DENY THEMSELVES, TAKE UP THEIR CROSS, AND IDENTIFY THEMSELVES WITH
HIS NEW COMMUNITY.   THE RESULTS OF EVANGELISM INCLUDE OBEDIENCE TO CHRIST,
INCORPORATION INTO HIS CHURCH AND RESPONSIBLE SERVICE IN THE WORLD.

... Sharing Jesus

NEW FILM SERIES BEGINS IN MAY
Further Details Inside

2. Copy Set in Capital Letters

PATHFINDER NEWS

Our Pathfinder Club is off and rolling once again! Last Tuesday evening Sept 29 saw 21 eager Pathfinders show up for our first meeting of the year. They are a joyous and enthusiastic bunch...The cream of the crop!

This year we are meeting on Tuesday evening from 6:30 til 8:00. We have some new classes this year: Ray Cress will be teaching a class in Mammals and Reptiles; Beverly Farley is teaching a class in Insects; and Lynn Plafkr is teaching a class in Bread Dough craft. Our first outing this year will be the Pathfinder Camporee at Los Cayotes on the weekend of OCT. 16-18. It promises to be a real blessing and lots of fun. On Halloween the Club will be contacting our community requesting donations of canned goods and non perishable items instead of candy etc. These goods will be placed in needy homes on or around Thanksgiving. We have some exciting activities in the planning stage: a possible Christmas Program, an outing to the desert in January or February, and also a snow day.

It promises to be a full and exciting year. Please keep our club and staff before the Lord in your prayers.

3. Copy Set in Italics

THE CHURCH MOUSE

A word of thanks goes to BIRCHIE COX at BIRCHIE'S FLOWERS for the carnations last week. She plans to donate carnations each Sunday for the ushers and staff members. We also want to express our appreciation to BUDDY BICE & PAT'S FLORIST for the beautiful flowers they donate for the sanctuary every Sunday...Brotherhood Breakfast next Sunday morning. LAWRENCE HAMMOND, Glen Rose camp manager will be the speaker...Baptism was observed both services last Sunday morning and will be observed both services again next Sunday morning..We will observe the Lord's Supper during both services on Sunday morning, July 25.. E.E. Blitz sign-up will be this coming Sunday morning, July 18...Our youth will present the musical, "The Witness" Sunday night during the evening worship service..Pray for a safe return for our youth as they come home from Nebraska this weekend...Our new church training groups got off to a great start last Sunday. Perhaps you need to be in one of them this coming Sunday at 5:45...We will have Baby Dedication service during the 11:00 worship this Sunday. If you would like to participate, please call the church office....It's time to sign up for the fall semester of Evangelism Explosion...Afternoon at the Ballfield will be enjoyed Sunday afternoon, July 25....Plan to attend our all-church family retreat Labor Day weekend. It starts Sunday afternoon at 3:30 and we will come home Monday about

Keeping Up With Our Fellowship

—Ron and Margaret Whitworth Romeis have a baby daughter, Sarah Ellen, born in Philadelphia.

—Dr. and Mrs. Arthur Gray have a baby son, Matthew Robinson, in Augusta.

—Steve and Ann Ragsdale Gundry have a new baby daughter, Melissa Hickson, in Michigan.

—Edna Burns' father, Mr. Daniel Snyder, passed away on Friday, March 5th in Rome.

—Marvin Ryals, brother-in-law of Kate Strain and Leroy Strain, passed away in Stone Mountain.

--Linda Stevens has been initiated into the Phi Lamba Sigma Society at Auburn University where she is a senior in the School of Pharmacy.

4. Copy Crowded, No Eye Breaks

Travel- Carl and Lucille Hildreth are spending a part
ling   of this month in South Texas.

Appre-   To Desmond Bittinger for preaching and teach-
ciation ing the Questers' Bible Class on Feb. 7; to
         John Harshbarger for vacuuming up the water
in the carpet in the education building caused from a
backed up sewer; to our choir for providing special
music at the North Park Service of Prayer for Christian
Unity; to Ken & Mary Aeschbacher, Carmen & Gladden Boaz,
Pat & Tom Perry, and Irven & Pattie Stern for providing
hospitality to members of the Hispanic Network in Jan.

Volunteers Stewards Commission is seeking volunteers
Needed   to provide lawn care this year. Sign up
             for a month on the sheet in the south nar-
thex. Ask another family to share the month with you.
Sign up to prepare worship centers on the altar for
one or more Sundays this year. The sheet is in the
south narthex. Provide transportation to church for
someone who needs a ride. Contact the Beckwiths or
Wengers.

Bible Are you interested in being a part of a weekday
Study Bible study? Contact Jean McGary if you are.
       She is investigating to see if there is interest.

Annual Women from the Southern half of
Spring the Pacific Southwest Confer-
Rally   ence will gather at the Pasa-
        dena Church of the Brethren on
March 13 for a Women's Fellowship Annual
Spring Rally. It will begin at 9:30
a.m. and close at 3 p.m. The theme is
"Go With God--Let Our Lights Shine".
Those who plan to attend should give $4
for lunch and registration to Jean
McGary or Lucille Hildreth by Feb. 28.

Women's
News

Women A film and speaker on HOSPICE will be the fea-
To   ture of our local Women's Fellowship when they
Meet   meet in the sanctuary at 7 p.m., Mon., March 15.

6

Effective Use of Headlines in a Mimeographed Newsletter

BRAZIL MISSION TRIP

Church Parking Lot

Closed

To High School Drivers

Choir Presents Cantata Palm Sunday

John W. Peterson's "THE GLORY OF EASTER," will be presented by the Chancel Choir, Palm Sunday, April 12. Nancy Fox is director and Lloyd Geissinger, organist. Palms will be distributed to all worshipers at the close of the service that marks the beginning of Holy Week.

Council To Plan For Year Ahead

Improvements Needed

YOUNG ADULTS TO VISIT MISSIONARIES IN HAITI

Baptist Women Elect New President

Religious books needed for library

V.B.S. Sets New Record Attendance With 750 Present

PASTOR CONTINUES SPECIAL SERIES

Good Newsletter Headlines

BLOOD OF JESUS

The Blood of Jesus
will ever flow,
Wherever justice, mercy,
and love must go.

His Precious Blood
He did give,
So that in eternity
we might live.

With every drop of His Blood
He shed a tear,
That men might be free from sin
without any fear.

For this He suffered
with nails in each hand,
Hung high on a cross
above the land.

And in His side
He took a spear,
While the earth shook
and darkness did appear.

Saviour, Son of God,
You are the True One.
Forgive me for the evil
that I have done.

In Your Holy Blood
my soul is bathed,
It becomes pure and clean,
and thus is saved.

(Inspired by St. Catherine of Siena)
11/14/78

GET TO KNOW OTHER FBC'ers
This Saturday evening at six o'clock in Fellowship Hall, adults of all ages are invited to a covered-dish supper. A brief fellowship-program will follow the meal. Then everyone will be asked to join a group of adults who will meet once a month for three months in a home for covered-dish meals and fellowship.

This is a wonderful way for new members and "old" members to get acquainted. So come Saturday night with a covered-dish. If you need the preschool nursery provided, phone 534-5646.

Simple But Effective Art Treatments

LORD, HELP US!

Dear Lord,

I want to serve you so badly! I'm literally burning with the fever. I've been on vacation and I'm more ready than I've ever been. What I need now is an assignment. That's what I want to discuss with you.

I've been offered the position of program chairperson for the women at the church, but I'm hoping you'll agree with me that it's not quite right. They need a teacher badly in the Junior Department of the Sunday School, but I know too many of the children. Wild bunch if I ever saw one (but it's no wonder, considering the homes they come from). I would love to help out in the nursery, but that would mean missing the worship service occasionally, and I know you would not want me to do that. Besides, my children are too old for the nursery. The woman next door can't drive. She needs help with the groceries and she needs company, but she never lets go once she gets hold of you.

How about something different? No nursing homes, please; I can't stand some of what I see in those places.

I know you'll think of something. I can hardly wait.

With all my love,
Ima Servant
--copied

PLEASE READ ON . . .

As our Nominating Committee prayerfully seeks workers for the coming church year, a lot of already busy people will be asked to assume a place of responsibility. It is no trouble for all of us to find enough to keep busy. The real question is, "where will we be busy, and for whom?" When God wants a great servant, He calls a busy person. Both scripture and history attest to this truth.

If you have been thinking about where your talents could best serve your Lord, contact Pastor Schwein. He will be working with the Nominating Committee during September to find those who will support the ministry of the church by their willingness to help.

FAREWELL FOR AMY THOMAS

As announced in our last newsletter, Amy Thomas will conclude her duties as Youth Minister this month. She will be giving full time attention to her studies at IUPUI. We wish her well! An informal time for expressing gratitude and good wishes will be held on Sunday, August 22, beginning at 9:50 a.m.

A replacement for Amy will be announced sometime in August.

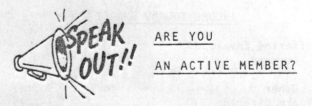

ARE YOU

AN ACTIVE MEMBER?

Remember the vow about upholding the church in your prayers, your presence, your gifts and your service?

SUMC apportionments are based in part on our church membership and we presently carry over 50 non-resident members and older youth for which we have no address. Someone has to pay their share of denominational askings. At the present, approximately $53 is paid for each member of the church.

If you (or your child) have moved to another state, or joined another church, please notify the church office so that our records may be updated.

 KEEP

IN

TOUCH

The church office would like to have the address of those who will be attending college in order to keep in touch with the monthly newsletter.

Please call the church office this fall as soon as an address is available.

Page with Right Mixture of Art and Copy

DEACON OF THE WEEK

Roy and Emma Lou Sheumaker met in the Singles Department here at Trinity Baptist. Roy joined TBC in 1953, Emma Lou joined in 1950. They have five children and six grand-children. Roy has taught for 29 years in the Sunday School at TBC, Emma Lou has taught the 1st graders for 21 years. Roy has now retired from a job with the city of Lubbock.

KITCHEN KORNER

WE NEED SOMEONE TO TAKE OVER IN THE KITCHEN! Jack and Linda Mace are being transferred to Tennessee and will be leaving us very soon, so we are looking for a replacement for Linda as Church Hostess. If you are interested, call the church office (799-4329).

WMU COUNCIL – the WMU Council will be meeting on Sunday, October 31 at 4:00 p.m. The nursery will be provided. All ladies that are involved with this council please be present.

ADULT CHOIR IS LOOKING FOR

YOU!!!

The Adult Choir is looking for new choir members. Won't you join us on Wednesday night in the choir room. NEW TIME-7:00.

Youth News

Tuesday, November 2nd, will be a VERY SPECIAL "Kidnap Visitation and Skate Party" for all Jr. and Sr. High. The fun begins at 6:00 p.m., so bring $1.00 and meet in the church parlor!

PLAN NOW to Attend...

BSU LUNCHEON -- All Baptist Women are invited to join in the fun and fellowship as food is prepared and served at the BSU on campus. A nursery will be provided at the church. Everyone is needed to meet at 8:30 a.m. on Thursday, November 4th at the church.

THANKS

"Thank You" notes have been received this week from: Ruth and Johny Johnson, the Gunn family, Ed Hollinsworth and family, Bertie Thompson and Evelyn Young, Gladys and E.C. Pool, and Janie Herrin.

Welcome to NEW MEMBERS

ACCEPTS CHRIST – BAPTISM

Johnny Bradshaw
3307 77th
Lubbock 79423

Bob Rezaee
3102 4th #54
Lubbock 79415

LETTER

James Childs
223 Indiana Ave. #B208
Lubbock 79415

Jency Thoma
2310 70th #111
Lubbock 79412

REDEDICATION

Cheryl Cypert
4415 39th
Lubbock 79414

Page with Too Much Art

The PRAYER SERVICE discontinued, Monday, 7:30 p.m., is due to over the We invite join with us share ing of prayer. If you have never been to a Prayer Service, come and see. We won't bite.

will be temporarily and will resume on February 1, at in the Church. This the small turnout past several weeks. the Parishioners to on February 1, and together an even-

Never "Jump" Type Over a Small Illustration

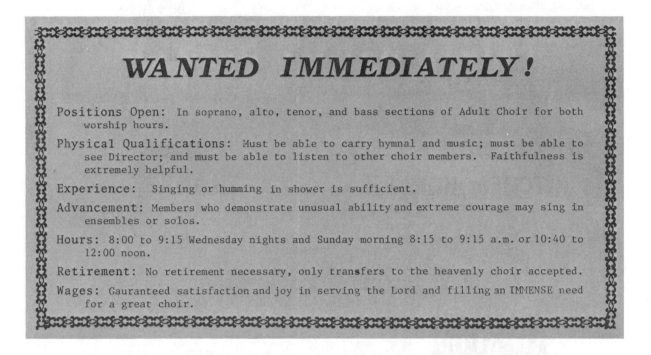

WANTED IMMEDIATELY!

Positions Open: In soprano, alto, tenor, and bass sections of Adult Choir for both worship hours.

Physical Qualifications: Must be able to carry hymnal and music; must be able to see Director; and must be able to listen to other choir members. Faithfulness is extremely helpful.

Experience: Singing or humming in shower is sufficient.

Advancement: Members who demonstrate unusual ability and extreme courage may sing in ensembles or solos.

Hours: 8:00 to 9:15 Wednesday nights and Sunday morning 8:15 to 9:15 a.m. or 10:40 to 12:00 noon.

Retirement: No retirement necessary, only transfers to the heavenly choir accepted.

Wages: Gauranteed satisfaction and joy in serving the Lord and filling an IMMENSE need for a great choir.

CHURCH FAMILY
THANKSGIVING
SUPPER

Tuesday, November 24
5:00-6:00 P.M.

Reservation deadline:
Monday at Noon

PRESCHOOL
CHRISTMAS PARTY
Ages 3-5 years
Saturday, December 12
10:00 — 11:15 a.m.
Fellowship Hall

Small Boxes: Attention-Getting Visual Elements

57

Dale Taylor Shares Tithing Testimony

Dale Taylor

Tithing is easy! The hard part is getting started! At least, this has been my experience. I can remember struggling with the issue many times as a single adult, and everytime I increased my giving I found that enough remained to meet my financial needs. This is not to say that I could not have found places to spend more money. I guess we could all do that! However, I don't think I could have spent it in a fashion that provided more personal satisfaction.

I used to think somehow that tithing would get easier when my income level increased; therefore, I continued to postpone what I knew was the right thing for me to do. In retrospect, the income level was not the issue. The issue was the willingness to make the commitment!

Tithing began for me after I married. Once the commitment was made, giving became much easier. In fact, it sometimes became too easy when I would forget that tithing involved more than just money and that it was in essence nothing more than what the Old Testament Law required. There was such a thing as "second-mile" giving.

Psalm 1:24 tells me that "The earth is the Lord's, and everything in it, the world, and all who live in it"; and Romans 14:8 says, "If we live, we live to the Lord; and if we die, we die to the Lord. So, whether we live or die, we belong to the Lord." These two verses put things in perspective for me: I wasn't really giving up anything I "owned" when I tithed my time, gifts, or money. God owns it all and graciously gives to us freely all things.

This is the work of a loving God who will help us to grow in His grace as we grow in our giving. After all, God understands Truth - as in, "It is really more blessed to give than to receive." In modern phraseology that says to me that giving, rather than receiving and keeping, is just a happier way to live!

College Department Welcomes New Directors, Outreach Leaders

On Sunday, 10 January of this year the college ministry of First Baptist Church received a charitable "booster shot" with the addition of Lyndon and Jan Herrstrom as new directors and W.L. and Cynthia McCulloch as new outreach leaders. During the past several weeks they have been working hard at learning names and getting acquainted with students and leadership.

When combined with the experience and dedication of the current college leadership, their enthusiasm and vitality produce a team of workers determined to serve the Lord with students within our church grasp.

Lyndon and Jan Herrstrom met several years ago at First Baptist Church in Dallas, Tx. where Jan was working with the media operations of the church. They married shortly thereafter and have two children Eric, 5 and Sue Allice, 8 months old. Raised in Illinois, Lyndon was graduated from Milwaukee School of Engineering and Purdue University. He is currently Facilities Manager for Mostek, Corp. in Carrolton, Texas. He is also Regional Education Chairman of The Society of Manufacturing Engineers and is a recently ordained deacon at our church. Jan is a native of Corpus Christi, Texas and was graduated from Baylor University with degrees in Journalism and English. She is currently a homemaker.

W.L. and Cynthia McCulloch are both natives of Arkansas and both are graduates of the University of Arkansas. In 1970, shortly after commencement, they were married and have three daughters Erin, 9 Kara, 6 and Lucy, 2 years of age. W.L. holds a bachelors and masters degree in mechanical engineering and is currently a Consulting Engineer specializing in the design of heating, air conditioning and plumbing systems for buildings, hotels, condominiums and hospitals. Cynthia has a degree in Home Economics and is practicing her training as a homemaker. They came to F.B.C. from First Baptist in Little Rock, Ark. W.L. is also a newly ordained deacon.

Please be in prayer for these new leaders as they develop student leadership and plan with their team of workers to establish the finest student ministry possible. Under God, we know such possibilities are assured. Welcome Lyndon, Jan, W.L. and Cynthia.

Seated: Cynthia McCulloch, Jan Herrstrom
Standing: W.L McCulloch, Lyndon Herrstrom

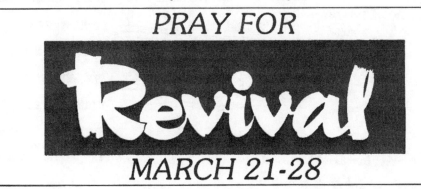

PRAY FOR Revival MARCH 21-28

First Baptist Church, Arlington
KTVT - Channel 11
Sunday - 9:30 to 10:00 A.M.

Too Much Copy Crowded on a Page

The Junior Choir sang beautifully at their annual visitation to the Cranford Hall Nursing Home on the evening of December 21st, and it was an inspiration to see them mingle with the patients, greeting them with conversation and Christmas wishes. The march through the halls singing Christmas songs was well received. John Horsley read the Christmas lesson impressively. Then all proceeded to the home of John and Jeanne (Cooper) Fitzgerald for socializing and goodies. Thanks Juniors and mothers who came with them for a lesson in Christian love and compassion.

On December 23rd, these young choristers also presented a chancel drama, Christmas 2001, a Christmas play in which all performed well, under the direction of Clinton Heyer, our Choirmaster, and Tom Cornell, Director.

Our Seniors worked hard and long in preparation for the Christmas music which we believe was well received at the two services on Christmas Day and the Midnight service on Christmas Eve.

Junior alumni members Betsy Mackenzie and Betty Kisner, the younger, visited the choir room after the Christmas Eve service, recalling their past association with us. Betsy is furthering her undoubted musical talent at Westminster College,

while Betty is a staff nurse at the Harvard Community Hospital in Boston. Thanks for dropping in, young ladies, we wish others would do it.

Sue Hull and Fern Bunting sang in a concert given by the Choral Art Society of Westfield, on January 12th. Two fine ladies added their pleasing voices to a superior choral group. Congratulations and well done, Fern and Sue!

Our good wishes also go to Jeff Roberts, who is moving to Lakewood, where he will soon be married to Donna Bunting. Jeff has returned to us his choir robe, after removing the St.Dunstan guild emblem he was given. He is the second person to be honored from our choir with membership in the Guild of St. Dunstan. Walter Cooper was the first to receive this membership from Trinity.

DON'T FORGET TO MARK YOUR CALENDARS FOR THE WEDNESDAY NIGHT LENTEN SUPPERS...Details will be given in the Parish Herald

Not Enough Copy on the Page

CDC Review

The five-year old children recently visited the Knoxville Convalescent and Nursing Home for Valentine. They sang five Valentine songs — "Love To You," "Love Somebody, Yes We Do," etc. The residents were so pleased, and the children had a delightful time. Some could only wave from their beds, but others came into the hallway in wheelchairs, but their smiles spoke deep appreciation. The children also went into the assembly rooms on both floors. It was a wonderful experience for us all. There was a little lady 95 years old rolling along in her wheelchair and singing with the children. She asked if she could lead them in singing "Jesus Loves Me." They followed her very well, enjoying singing with her. Even though they were ill, these residents enjoyed the children's singing and smiles, and as we left they heartily waved goodby.

The following week we visited the Brakebill Nursing Home and celebrated Mrs. Myrtle Reynolds birthday with her. We enjoyed our time there with her and other residents at Brakebill. The children made beautiful napkins for the people, which pleased them very much.

Jean Turner

MARRIAGE ENRICHMENT RETREAT

Our pastor, and his wife, Carol, will host the Marriage Enrichment Retreat in their home on Saturday, February 27, beginning at 6:00 p.m. Couples planning to attend should turn their names in to Adult I or Adult II Sunday School Departments no later than next Sunday. Rev. Bob Money, First Baptist Church, Knoxville, is to lead the Retreat. A pot luck dinner will be served at 6:30 p.m. This will be a choice spiritual experience for those in attendance.

North Knoxville Group Ministry Quarterly Fellowship

Mardi Gras Party at St. James Episcopal Church
Tuesday, February 23, 6:30 p.m.
Covered Dish Dinner

Special Guest: Kevin Leavy, Director of Columbus Home, Knoxville

Broadway and Oakwood in a Growing Challenge Campaign

Two of Knox County's great churches will engage in a six-weeks Sunday School campaign from **MARCH 7** through **APRIL 11**. Called **A GROWING CHALLENGE CAMPAIGN**, it is surely understood that the campaign will not create a loser in any true sense, but the challenge for both the Broadway Sunday School and that of Oakwood is intended to send us forth in an effort to reach and teach God's word to more people every week. However, as an inspiration to both these great Sunday Schools, **points of challenge** will be given each week, allowing the accumulation of points to determine the so-called "winner" after the six weeks. The four points of challenge are:

1. Points for enrollment percentage in attendance: 85% + = **25 points**; 70 - 84% = **20 points**; 50 - 69% = **15 points**, PLUS the S. S. with the best percent each week will earn a bonus **5 points**.

2. Each new member enrolled in either of the Sunday Schools earns **20 points**.

3. Each visitor present in either Sunday School will earn **15 points**.

4. Each home visit made and reported will earn **10 points**.

A SPIRITUAL WORK IS THE KEY

This is certainly not intended to be just "another contest." It is a call to the entire Sunday School to be about the Great Commission, doing a spiritual work of evangelizing, making disciples of all nations, and teaching God's revelation for all men. It is a call to make spiritual preparation for our **SPRING REVIVAL** set for April 4-11, which concludes the six-week campaign. We could refer to this effort as our "SPRING ROUNDUP" of all members and prospective members. Indeed, it is all of these things, but it is also a great way to learn more about another local church body, Oakwood Baptist.

Remember, the contest begins on Sunday, March 7, only three weeks hence. Sunday School leaders, begin NOW to make specific visitation assignments, be in touch each week with every absentee, and seek to enlist new members. The church is commissioned to reach out to every man, to share God's love and written Word with them. This we ought to do even without a campaign. God waits on us to be serious about Bible study that is coupled with direct evangelistic efforts. The lost also wait for us. To do less is to fail both our Lord and the lost.

Notice!

The Sign Language Class will have a new teacher, Ms. Patty Cistal, who teaches at T.S.D. She will be starting Thursday, February 18 at 7:00 p.m. Meeting place is the church library.

Just the Right Amount of Copy on the Page

TALKING HANDS

Saturday, February 27 — Clean Up, room 313, 9:30 a.m. Lunch will be served.

Sunday, February 28 — Banana Split Fellowship. Make your own banana split after the worship service Sunday night in the small dining room.

Friday, March 5 — Newspaper Night!!! Bring your newspapers to the FLC gym at 7:00 p.m. for an evening of fun.

INTERESTED IN SOFTBALL?

Entry deadline for softball is March 14. If you are interested in playing on one of the FBC teams, make plans to attend the spring sign-up session on March 9, 7:00 p.m., in the blue room of the Family Life Center. Teams for 1982 will consist of Men's Slow Pitch and Mixed Slow Pitch.

"Satan dreads nothing but prayer...The one concern of the devil is to keep the saints from prayer. He fears nothing from prayerless studies, prayerless work, prayerless religion. He laughs at our toil, mocks at our wisdom, but trembles when we pray."

Shown above is Mrs. Mary Rippy who celebrated her 90th birthday on February 19. Mrs. Rippy lives at 2409 S. Polk.

Congratulations to Mrs. Rippy and may the Lord continue His blessings on her during this year.

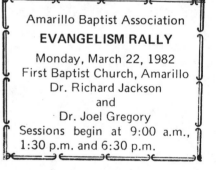

Amarillo Baptist Association
EVANGELISM RALLY
Monday, March 22, 1982
First Baptist Church, Amarillo
Dr. Richard Jackson
and
Dr. Joel Gregory
Sessions begin at 9:00 a.m.,
1:30 p.m. and 6:30 p.m.

(AMERICA, page 1)

pons. This young Roman Catholic had been sent here by his paper to write a story for the rest of the country about the feelings and the reactions, especially of the religious community, on this subject. I tried to share with him what I've been reading with you from the Book of Joshua, of God's command to His people concerning those who occupied the land of Canaan, and in their sin and arrogance had refused to repent. And God said, "Wipe them out." It was the last resort. I spoke with him about God's command to Saul through the prophet Samuel, concerning the total annihilation of the Amalakites. Then I remembered that Jesus, the Prince of Peace, never taught that there can be "peace at any price." In the tenth chapter of Matthew, He said even those who follow Him will discover that He did not come to bring peace but to send a sword. Peace is sweet. Freedom is sweeter. Nonconflict is desirable. But the proclamation of the saving knowledge of Christ is the essential thing!

No, I am not a pacifist, and I am not neutral. I am for America. I am for a strong America because I do believe that the hope of the world is here, and that whatever peace time we have, we must use it to proclaim the Gospel of Jesus Christ to all the world.

Mr. Jim Franklin, of Boston, said to me, as he was leaving, "I will send you a copy of my story and our interview. Sir, what you people think, feel, and do here is far more important than you could possibly know. You live here where the weapons are being assembled. We are out there in the rest of the country waiting to see how you feel and what you do."

I **assured him** of this one thing, that whatever views we hold in this city and area concerning nuclear weapons and Bishop Matthiesen's invitation for people to leave their jobs for conscience's sake, we will not allow any of this to fracture our fellowship and disrupt the harmonious way of life we have enjoyed as citizens of this community. We have all worked hard for many years to build relationships and to keep them Christian. No difference of personal opinion is going to rob us of that in Amarillo.

I'll see you in all the services of the Lord's Day.

CHRISTIAN SYMPATHY

Christian sympathy is extended to the family of Mrs. W. C. Rogers in her death; to Mr. Cleon Ligon in the death of his uncle; to Mrs. Helen Christianson in the death of her mother; to Mrs. James Burgtorf in the death of her father-in-law; to Mrs. Gordon Blackburn in the death of her sister, and Miss Margaret Blackburn in the death of her aunt; to Mrs. L. O'Brien Thompson in the death of her aunt to Mr. Jarrett Ransom in the death of his mother; to Mr. LeeRoy Pee' in the death of his sister; to Mr. Howard Wilson in the death of his brother; to Mrs. Birk Graham in the death of her husband; to Mrs. Ellen Barksdale in the death of her brother-in-law; to Mrs. Don Holtzclaw in the death of her sister-in-law.

Strongest Visual Elements Jammed Together

"Satan dreads nothing but prayer...The one concern of the devil is to keep the saints from prayer. He fears nothing from prayerless studies, prayerless work, prayerless religion. He laughs at our toil, mocks at our wisdom, but trembles when we pray."

TALKING HANDS

Saturday, February 27 — Clean Up, room 313, 9:30 a.m. Lunch will be served.

Sunday, February 28 — Banana Split Fellowship. Make your own banana split after the worship service Sunday night in the small dining room.

Friday, March 5 — Newspaper Night!!! Bring your newspapers to the FLC gym at 7:00 p.m. for an evening of fun.

INTERESTED IN SOFTBALL?

Entry deadline for softball is March 14. If you are interested in playing on one of the FBC teams, make plans to attend the spring sign-up session on March 9, 7:00 p.m., in the blue room of the Family Life Center. Teams for 1982 will consist of Men's Slow Pitch and Mixed Slow Pitch.

Shown above is Mrs. Mary Rippy who celebrated her 90th birthday on February 19. Mrs. Rippy lives at 2409 S. Polk.

Congratulations to Mrs. Rippy and may the Lord continue His blessings on her during this year.

CHRISTIAN SYMPATHY

Christian sympathy is extended to the family of Mrs. W. C. Rogers in her death; to Mr. Cleon Ligon in the death of his uncle; to Mrs. Helen Christianson in the death of her mother; to Mrs. James Burgtorf in the death of her father-in-law; to Mrs. Gordon Blackburn in the death of her sister, and Miss Margaret Blackburn in the death of her aunt; to Mrs. L. O'Brien Thompson in the death of her aunt to Mr. Jarrett Ransom in the death of his mother; to Mr. LeeRoy Pee' in the death of his sister; to Mr. Howard Wilson in the death of his brother; to Mrs. Birk Graham in the death of her husband; to Mrs. Ellen Barksdale in the death of her brother-in-law; to Mrs. Don Holtzclaw in the death of her sister-in-law.

(AMERICA, page 1)

pons. This young Roman Catholic had been sent here by his paper to write a story for the rest of the country about the feelings and the reactions, especially of the religious community, on this subject. I tried to share with him what I've been reading with you from the Book of Joshua, of God's command to His people concerning those who occupied the land of Canaan, and in their sin and arrogance had refused to repent. And God said, "Wipe them out." It was the last resort. I spoke with him about God's command to Saul through the prophet Samuel, concerning the total annihilation of the Amalakites. Then I remembered that Jesus, the Prince of Peace, never taught that there can be "peace at any price." In the tenth chapter of Matthew, He said even those who follow Him will discover that He did not come to bring peace but to send a sword. Peace is sweet. Freedom is sweeter. Nonconflict is desirable. But the proclamation of the saving knowledge of Christ is the essential thing!

No, I am not a pacifist, and I am not neutral. I am for America. I am for a strong America because I do believe that the hope of the world is here, and that whatever peace time we have, we must use it to proclaim the Gospel of Jesus Christ to all the world.

Mr. Jim Franklin, of Boston, said to me, as he was leaving, "I will send you a copy of my story and our interview. Sir, what you people think, feel, and do here is far more important than you could possibly know. You live here where the weapons are being assembled. We are out there in the rest of the country waiting to see how you feel and what you do."

I assured him of this one thing, that whatever views we hold in this city and area concerning nuclear weapons and Bishop Matthiesen's invitation for people to leave their jobs for conscience's sake, we will not allow any of this to fracture our fellowship and disrupt the harmonious way of life we have enjoyed as citizens of this community. We have all worked hard for many years to build relationships and to keep them Christian. No difference of personal opinion is going to rob us of that in Amarillo.

I'll see you in all the services of the Lord's Day.

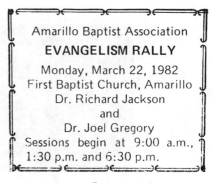

Amarillo Baptist Association
EVANGELISM RALLY
Monday, March 22, 1982
First Baptist Church, Amarillo
Dr. Richard Jackson
and
Dr. Joel Gregory
Sessions begin at 9:00 a.m.,
1:30 p.m. and 6:30 p.m.

Strongest Visual Elements Scattered for Maximum Eye Appeal

DECISIONS

BY PROFESSION OF FAITH
Rita Kay Alligood (AM2/L2)
656 Halifax Dr. 666-8872
Debbie Ashworth (AE01)
4015 A. Seabreeze Rd. 344-7323
Michelle Badon (PS5A)
5358 Timberline Rdg. 666-5825
Christi Glanz (C1E)
363 Azalea Rd. R-3 344-3585
Greg Jackson (AM01)
1632 Indian Trail Dr. 661-4595
Jeff Money (YL9B)
685 Tarawa Dr. 666-0649
Lisa Moore (8G)
656 Halifax Dr. 666-8872
Lonnie Rawlins (YL9B)
4382 Fathbrook Ln. 666-0653
Luc (Luke) Robert (SA01)
2451 Buena Dr. 471-4577
Robert Shackelford (AE1/AM1/AL1)
Linda Shackelford (AE1/AM1/AL1)
1555 S. Broad No. 13
Mark Stewart (C6D)
4001 Oxmoore 661-1633

BY LETTER/STATEMENT
Wayne Alligood (AM2)
656 Halifax Dr. 666-8872
Bertha J. Hubbard (SA7)
5513 Royal Oak Dr. 666-3502
Bernard Johnson (AM5)
Agnes Johnson (AM5)
3515 Riviere DuChien 661-5570
Edward Majure (AM1)
Cathy Majure (AM1)
375 Arnold Rd. C106 344-7603
Mary Lou Ray (SA5)
375 Arnold Rd. D102 344-9806
Linda Smith (SA3)
53 Cherry Dr. 675-1585
Robert (Pete) Wilkins (AM3)
Betty Wilkins (AM3)
4151 Spring Valley Dr. 666-4038

VITAL SIGNS

SUNDAY SCHOOL ATND 2359
   Adults. 857
   Youth & College 409
   Children. 587
   Preschool. 506

CHURCH TRAINING ATND 731

MISSION REPORT:
   Birdville. 33

Contribution Received:
• For Budget Allocations . . . $30,827.31
• Other Designations $3,859.02
• From God's Hands Commitments:
  Received this week $9,718.00
  Cash received to date . . . $520,900.92

The Challenge (USPS 133-900) is published
weekly, except the week of Christmas, by the
Cottage Hill Baptist Church, 4255 Cottage Hill
Road, Mobile, Ala. Second-class postage paid
at Mobile, Ala. 36609. Charles Wood, Editor.

NOTICE TO TAPE CUSTOMERS
Since Jan. 1, 1978, the price for our Sunday tapes with two messages have been $3.25. Due to the cost of materials, postage and other costs of equipment, we find it necessary to increase the price to $3.50, effective March 1, 1982. If you mailed, add 50 cents extra. If you have tapes that have been ordered for sometime and failed to pick them up, please do so at your earliest convenience.

B. C. Jones

MOVIE DISCOUNT
The Bel Air Cinema in Mobile is to be commended for two films scheduled for showing in March: "Chariots of Fire" beginning March 5 and "Joni" starting March 19.

"Chariots of Fire" is based on history: two runners who represented Great Britain in the Paris Olympics of 1924. Eric Liddell, a devout Scottish Evangelical, runs to bring glory to God. Inspiration Films is offering a toll free number - 1-800-423-5509 for those who want to order 5 or more advance discount tickets. The advance discount savings amounts to approx. $2.00 per adult ticket.

NOTES OF APPRECIATION
Thank you for your concern, acts of love, shown us at the death of our Father.

The Greg Moe Family

I want to thank all the faithful and staff for the many visits, cards, calls and flowers during my recent stay in the hospital. Each was a rich source of spiritual uplift. Thank you again.
Mrs.

CHRISTIAN SYMPATHY
To the Family of Charles Breland, in the death of Mr. Ronald Allen Breland.
AND
To the Family of Mrs. in the death of her Sister,
AND
To the Family of Mr. in the death of his Richardson.

BIBLE VERSE FOR THE WEEK

This week: Feb. 14-20
I John 4:7: "Beloved, let us love one another: for love is of God; and every one that loveth is born of God, and knoweth God."
Next week: Feb. 21-27
I John 4:13: "Hereby know we that we dwell in him, and he in us, because he hath given us of his Spirit."

BIBLE READINGS

Two Approaches to the "Catch-All" Page

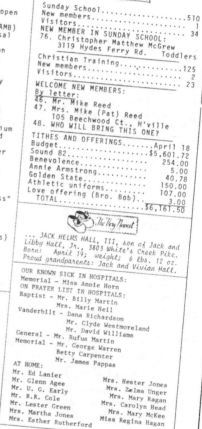

Opportunities for the Week

SUNDAY - April 25
  9:00-9:30 AM - Media Center open
  9:30 AM - Sunday School
  11:00 AM - Morning Worship (WAMB)
  5:00 PM - Youth Choir rehearsal
  5:30 PM - Media Center open
  5:30 PM - Evangelism Explosion
  6:00 PM - Christian Training
  7:00 PM - Evening Worship
TUESDAY - April 27
  9:00 AM-2:00 PM - Mother's Day Out
  7:00 PM - Visitation
WEDNESDAY - April 28
  5:30-6:30 PM - GRACE ON VIACOM TV, CHANNEL 23
  5:45-5:50 PM - Meet in auditorium for announcements and blessing
  5:50-6:25 PM - Fellowship supper
  6:30-7:10 PM - S.S. dir. mtg.
  6:30-7:10 PM - S.S. teach. mtg.
  6:30-7:10 PM - Adult Enrichment Study (by Gail Green and Ann Zimmerle) Subject: "Media Madness"
  6:25-7:05 PM - Acteens, GA's, RA's, Mission Friends
  7:10-7:50 PM - Graded Choirs
  7:15-7:45 PM - Prayer meeting (Media/Library emphasis)
  7:55 PM - Church Choir rehearsal
THURSDAY - April 29
  9:00 AM-2:00 PM - Mother's Day Out
SATURDAY - April 30
  10:00 AM - Women's softball

Thank You

To the members of Grace Church:
Thanks so much for remembering me in prayer, with your visits, calls and cards during my recent stay in the hospital.
Inez Short
(mother of Marie Phillips)

A special word of thanks to Mrs. Gustave Ahrenhold for the two lovely matching floral arrangements in our sanctuary last Sunday. They were from the funeral flowers of Mr. Ahrenhold.

MENU
APRIL 28
Baked Chicken
Mashed Potatoes   Green Beans
SURPRISE   Rolls
Volunteer Hostess...Loretta Johnson

MORE WAY TO SOW GRASS AT GRACE SCHEDULED TO SATURDAY, MAY 1

The Record Speaks

Sunday School. 510
New members. 1
Visitors. 34
NEW MEMBER IN SUNDAY SCHOOL:
76. Christopher Matthew McGrew
3119 Hydes Ferry Rd. Toddlers

Christian Training. 125
New members. 5
Visitors. 23

WELCOME NEW MEMBERS:
By letter:
46. Mr. Mike Reed
47. Mrs. Mike (Pat) Reed
105 Beechwood Ct., H'ville
48. WHO WILL BRING THIS ONE?

TITHES AND OFFERINGS:
Budget. . . . . .April 18
Sound 82. . . . . $5,601.72
Benevolence. 254.00
Annie Armstrong. 5.00
Golden State. 40.78
Athletic uniforms. 150.00
Love offering (Bro. Bob). 107.00
   TOTAL. $6,161.50

The Very Newest

... JACK HELMS HALL, III, son of Jack and Libby Hall, Jr., 3805 White's Creek Pike. Born: April 19; weight; 6 lbs. 12 oz. Proud grandparents: Jack and Vivian Hall.

OUR KNOWN SICK IN HOSPITALS:
Memorial - Miss Annie Horn
ON PRAYER LIST IN HOSPITALS:
Baptist - Mr. Billy Martin
       Mrs. Marie Heil
Vanderbilt - Dana Richardson
       Mr. Clyde Westmoreland
       Mr. David Williams
General - Mr. Rufus Martin
Memorial - Mr. George Warren
       Betty Carpenter
       Mr. James Pappas
AT HOME:
Mr. Ed Lanier   Mrs. Hester Jones
Mr. Glenn Agee   Mrs. Zelma Unger
Mr. U. G. Early   Mrs. Mary Ragan
Mr. R.R. Cole   Mrs. Carolyn Head
Mr. Lester Green   Mrs. Mary McKee
Mrs. Martha Jones   Miss Regina Hagan
Mrs. Esther Rutherford

Sympathy
... To Mrs. J. Roy Bethune and family in the death of Bro. Roy Bethune.
... To the family of Mr. Billy Driver.

TIME CHANGE SATURDAY, APRIL 24
SET YOUR CLOCKS FORWARD ONE HOUR

THE INFORMER
First Baptist Church

FIRST BAPTIST
Missions Weekend

Newsletter Printed on Dark-Colored Paper

5
Preparing the Master:
Stencil and Paste-up Tips

No matter how you print your newsletter—by mimeograph, offset, or copying machine—you have to begin with a master copy of the pages you want to reproduce. The standard mimeograph process requires that this master copy be made on a stencil. A paste-up is what you need if you print by any of the other processes.

How do you prepare a good stencil master or a good paste-up master for the pages of your church newsletter? The following tips should help you in this important part of the job.

How to Prepare a Stencil

Printing a newsletter with a stencil on a mimeograph machine will be a part of the production scene in churches for many years to come. True, offset printing and photocopying machines have come on strong in recent years. But mimeograph is still the system with the edge when it comes to price. And mimeograph is not as messy as it used to be. Even hassle-free printing in a second color is a possibility with some of the newer machines.

If you plan to stay with the stencil, you owe it to your church newsletter to squeeze every ounce of potential out of the mimeograph process. Think about investing in such stencil preparation aids as letterguides for tracing large headlines; marking instruments (known as *styli;* singular *stylus*) for the drawing letters and illustrations on the stencil; special grids for putting attention-getting shading behind blocks of copy; and a mimeo scope board for better stencil preparation.

The scope board consists of a light in a box beneath a sheet of glass. The operator places the stencil on this glass over a piece of art that he wants to copy. The glass provides a hard-working surface for flawless tracing.

Take a good look at illustrations of these stencil preparation aids on page 68 to get an idea of how they work. Most of these are probably available at your local mimeograph supplier. Or write the Gestetner Corporation, Yonkers, New York 10703 and ask for a copy of their catalog of stencil cutting aids.

Another piece of equipment that can help you produce a first-class stencil is an electric typewriter—preferably one with the pop-on "golf ball" element that allows you to change typefaces. With an electric typewriter, of course, you get a much more uniform impression on the stencil than you would with a manual model. And the interchangeable typeface feature enables you to prepare a stencil with a little more variety.

A combination of three different typefaces is ideal for most church newsletters (see illustration, p. 68). This newsletter uses the large type in capital letters for headlines, the second type for the main body copy, and the italics type, in small doses, for emphasis and variety. With this line-up of typewriter faces, all from the same flexible machine, you can put some real sparkle into your mimeographed newsletter pages.

For best results in stencil preparation, rough out the pages of your newsletter on blank sheets of paper before doing the stencil typing. This rough outline should show the location of all headlines and pieces of art. Then, using this rough sketch as a guide, mark the locations of all headlines and pieces of art on the blank stencil. Apply a light outline of correction fluid to the stencil to mark these locations. After typing the stencil, trace the headlines and artwork in these blank spaces that were marked for this purpose. If you're working with art in stencil form, cut out the blank sections of the stencil and replace them with the stencil art spots, attach them with cement, and apply correction fluid.

Before inserting the stencil in the typewriter, clean the keys of your machine with a chemical cleaner. And check the keys every page or two to make sure they remain free of dirt and grime. This assures you of a firm, even impression. Type one complete column on the stencil; then take it out and insert it again to type the next column. Never roll the stencil back and forth in the machine; this could cause it to tear or wrinkle.

Many typists have discovered that removing the plastic cover sheet and typing directly on the stencil yields a sharper impression. But here's another time-saving tip if you're using a carbon ribbon with an electric typewriter. Set your typewriter for a heavy impression and type directly through the ribbon onto the plastic cover sheet. This will leave a clean, black image—one that's much easier to proofread than the faint impression on the dark stencil surface.

To insert a stencil lengthwise into the typewriter, fold a sheet of paper in half, the long way, and place the stencil inside the fold. Then hold the stencil firmly between the folded sheet as you roll it into the machine. After the stencil is in place, pull the paper release and slide the sheet of paper slowly out of the machine, leaving the stencil firmly seated and free of wrinkles. Putting the stencil in lengthwise without this paper cover could tear the unprotected edge.

Making corrections on a stencil is a fine art that comes with practice. For best results, check for errors as you type and correct them as soon as they happen. To correct minor errors, cover the letters or words with thin coats of correction fluid. Then type right on top of this wax coating as soon as it dries. To make corrections involving several lines, cut out the faulty copy with a razor blade. Type the correction on a blank section of a discarded stencil. Then attach the new copy to the stencil with cement and correction fluid. Make sure this patch is thoroughly dry before placing the stencil on the mimeograph machine.

Cut out any blank, unused portions of your old stencils before throwing them away. These will come in handy later as correction patches and save your church money at the same time.

When typing one long article with many paragraphs on a stencil, remember to double space between the paragraphs. There's something about single-spaced typewritten copy that makes it look jammed together if it is typed solid without eye breaks between the paragraphs. Likewise, make sure the columns on the page don't run together. For an attractive look, newsletter columns should be separated by at least one fourth of an inch of space.

If you don't have a typewriter with a larger headline type, set your headlines in all capital letters and underline them (see illustration, p. 68). Notice that this newsletter also spaces between every letter in some of these headlines to give them even more contrast. But use this technique sparingly. It can get monotonous very quickly if used for every headline in the newsletter. Remember, too, to triple-space between words in the headlines if you use this letterspacing approach.

As we discussed in chapter 4, one of the best ways to dress up your newsletter is to enclose some of the features on the pages in borders and boxes. But how can you do this with a typewritten stencil? One quick and easy way is to use the asterisk key (*) on your typewriter (see illustration, p. 68). See how this creative newsletter editor typed a line of these characters all the way around this block of copy?

Other typewriter characters that could be used like this to make attractive borders on a stencil include the hyphen (-), the plus sign (+), the period (.), and the lowercase o. The dollar sign ($) might even be appropriate for some types of stewardship material in the church paper.

No discussion of stencil preparation would be complete without exploring an innovation known as the electronic stencil. More and more churches seem to be turning to this system to produce their newsletters and bulletins.

The electronic stencil is gaining in popularity because it eliminates the messy task of typing directly on a stencil. The newsletter editor types the copy on plain white paper, then assembles this material with headlines and artwork into a master paste-up. This paste-up is then placed on a machine known as the electronic stencil scanner. This scanner converts the paste-up into a standard stencil for use on your mimeograph machine (see photographs, p. 69).

The real beauty of the electronic stencil process is that it combines the flexibility of paste-up preparation with the high speed, low cost, and convenient operation of a mimeograph machine. The biggest expense of the system is the stencil scanner. In many cities local mimeograph suppliers will use their equipment to convert your paste-up into a stencil for a modest charge. You might check into this service if you want to avoid the cost of buying the scanner. Several churches in the same community could share the expense of buying one scanner. It could be kept in one centrally located church office with all churches using it as needed.

Still other churches have discovered that the electronic stencil process can give their newsletters a lavishly illustrated look at moderate expense. You could clip good illustrations from many noncopyrighted sources, including business bulletins and "junk mail." Tape these illustrations down on stencil-size sheets of paper with transparent tape. Have these sheets converted into stencil art by your local mimeo supplier on his stencil scanner. Then you could cut these pieces of art into your stencils as you need them. It's a great way to get some unusual art into your mimeographed newsletter.

This covers some of the basics of stencil preparation. Now let's explore some principles that can help you prepare a better paste-up for your church paper.

How to Prepare a Paste-up

Let's begin by defining the mysterious term. What exactly is a paste-up? It's a master copy of the pages of your newsletter from which reproductions are made. This master copy consists of headlines, copy, and illustrations—all arranged exactly the way you want them to appear when the church paper is printed. These various elements are "pasted-up" in permanent form so they will remain stationary while a plate is being made or the master image is being copied—thus the term *paste-up*.

Professional graphic artists have well-equipped studios with many time-saving tools for turning out paste-ups. You probably don't have this luxury in a church office. But even with a few bare essentials, you can do an acceptable paste-up for your church newsletter. The trick is in knowing what tools are absolutely necessary and how to use them to your greatest advantage.

Paste-up Tools

Preparing a newsletter paste-up really doesn't require a lot of working space. The top of your desk should be sufficient. If possible, buy a desk-top fluorescent lamp, the type that sits low and throws a flood of light all over the desk. This will make the close work that paste-up requires much easier on the eyes.

A desk pad with a replaceable cardboard mat is also ideal for paste-up work. Use this cardboard as a working surface. You can mark and cut this without marring the surface of your desk. If one of these is not available, a piece of cardboard about 30x24″ in size will serve the same purpose.

Other tools needed to turn out acceptable paste-ups include a pair of scissors; masking tape; transparent tape; a couple of felt-tip pens of different sizes with jet-black ink; a plastic, "see-through" ruler, 18″ long; a small pair of tweezers; a nonreproducible, light-blue pencil; a bottle of white correction fluid; an eraser; a sharp, pointed knife like an X-Acto knife for trimming copy and illustrations; and a small bottle of rubber cement with its own brush in the lid (see photo of these tools on p. 70). You probably already have many of these items in your office; the others can be purchased at office-supply or art-supply stores.

Another handy item that is well worth its modest cost is a preprinted layout sheet. You can paste your copy, headlines, and illustrations right down on this sheet, using its grid lines as guides to keep the page straight (see illustration, p. 71). This eliminates the need for T-squares, light tables, and other expensive tools that professionals use to keep their paste-ups in perfect alignment. Layout sheets are printed in nonreproducible, light-blue ink, so you don't have to worry about their grid patterns showing up when the newsletter is printed. Usually sold in pads of 50 or 100, layout sheets are available at art-supply stores or your local mimeograph dealer.

Basics of Paste-up

Following is the general procedure for preparing a paste-up of the pages for your newsletter. These steps are fully illustrated on page 72.

1. A good paste-up of a newsletter page begins with a rough sketch of what you think the page should look like. Estimate the amount of space the copy will fill, using the number of words in the copy as a guide for your projection. Also rough in any headlines, borders, and illustrations that will appear on the page.

2. Using this rough layout as a guide, type the copy, set the headlines, and assemble the artwork. Then cut these items out of the pieces of paper on which they have been composed. Trim these elements about one eighth of an inch from their printing edges so they will not overlap when placed down on the paste-up.

3. Next, outline the margins of a printed page for your newsletter on the preprinted layout sheet. Use the non-reproducible blue pencil to draw this outline. The box formed by these margin lines should be exactly the size of the printed portion of one of your newsletter pages. All copy, headlines, and illustrations must fit within this box. After you have drawn the margin lines, use a piece of masking tape or transparent tape to secure the layout sheet to your desk top or other working surface so it won't be sliding around.

4. Place the copy, headlines, and illustrations loosely on the layout sheet to see how they fit together. If you have too much copy, cut a paragraph from an article, eliminate a piece of artwork, or shorten a headline. If you don't have enough copy to fill the space, add a paragraph to an article or use another piece of artwork or a short filler. The object at this stage of the paste-up is to add, delete, or rearrange until all the elements fit together to form a pleasing and harmonious page. To make the page look just right, you may have to put it together a little differently than you projected on your rough layout sketch.

5. After deciding on the final page arrangement, use the rubber cement to attach the copy, headlines, and illustrations permanently to the layout sheet. The pair of tweezers comes in handy for handling small pieces of copy. Apply a thin coat of cement to the back of each piece of paper and press it carefully into place. Use the faint blue lines on the layout sheet as guides to make sure everything is pasted down straight.

One of the great qualities of rubber cement is that it doesn't set up for a few minutes. You can move the copy around even after you place it down until it's perfectly aligned. Then use the plastic see-through ruler to press all copy down firmly for a secure seal. The lines on this ruler are also useful as a gauge for checking the alignment of all elements in the paste-up.

6. Give the rubber cement about eight to ten minutes to set up firmly. Then use the eraser to remove any smudges, fingerprints, or excess cement that has dried on the surface of the layout sheet. Any stubborn smudges should be covered with white correction fluid. Dirt spots on the paste-up will reproduce as smudges on your newsletter pages, so make sure the paste-up is clean.

Paste-up Tips

The above six steps cover the essentials of paste-up, but there are many "little things" that can make this job much easier if you will keep them in mind. Paste-up professionals offer the following time-saving and work-saving tips.

1. Remember that the reproduction of your newsletter will be exactly like the master paste-up which you produce—a good example of the ancient principle, "What you see is what you get." This means you have to keep your paste-up neat and clean. Make sure your typewriter keys are clean when you type copy for the newsletter. Use an electric typewriter with a carbon ribbon for best results. And be sure to keep your hands clean while preparing the paste-up.

2. Always type copy and compose headlines for the newsletter on separate pieces of white paper. Then clip these out for final positioning on the page layout sheet. This allows you to move these elements around, as discussed in the basic steps above, until you decide on the most pleasing arrangement.

3. The practice of clipping items from other publications for reproduction in your newsletter can save time. But make sure this material is not copyrighted before you reproduce it. And remember that some colors of ink on certain colored paper stocks will not reproduce very well. Clippings in orange, green, or brown ink will not reproduce at all if they are printed on anything but white paper. But darker inks like black and red will usually reproduce well, even when printed on pastel-colored paper like yellow, buff, and ivory. Your best guarantee of flawless reproduction, of course, is to stick with clippings that are printed in black ink on white paper.

4. To take up copy or headlines that have been glued firmly to the layout sheet, use rubber cement thinner. Lift one edge of the piece of paper and apply a drop of the fluid, using a small brush or eyedropper. Peel the paper back by applying drops all along the edge as it lifts slowly off the layout sheet. The thinner will evaporate quickly without leaving any spots on the paste-up.

5. Use a felt-tip pen with jet-black ink to draw a box around a block of copy that you really want to emphasize in your layout. To draw a neat box, paste the copy down on a separate sheet of white paper. Use a straight edge and the felt-tip pen to draw a line on all four sides of the copy, overlapping the lines by about one inch at all four corners of the box. Then, with a pair of scissors, snip the lines at a 45° angle just above the points where they intersect (see illustration, p. 73). This produces a neat, ruled box that is ready to be pasted down on the newsletter layout sheet.

6. To center headlines in the middle of a box, use a ruler to find the center point of each line of type. Mark the centers with a nonreproducible blue pencil. Then find the center of the box and draw a vertical line down the middle with this special pencil. Now you can center the headlines easily by lining up these two marks as you glue the copy down line by line (see illustrations, p. 73).

7. Here's a quick way to divide a ruled box into equal sections for time-saving layout and paste-up. Place the left end of a ruler (at its beginning point) against the upper left edge of the box. Then lower the right end of the ruler along the right edge of the box until it reaches a number that is easily divisible by the number of sections you want the box to contain. For example, if you want to divide the box into three sections, stop the ruler at 9″ near the bottom of the right-hand side. Then mark the paper with your nonreproducible blue pencil at each three-inch interval along the ruler (see illustration, p. 74). This divides the box quickly and easily into three equal parts.

This little technique will also work if you want to divide your newsletter layout sheets into several equal parts. Some-times the "dividing game" can help you as you try to work out a balanced arrangement for all the diverse elements that make up the pages of your newsletter.

Transfer-Type Headlines

Composing transfer-type headlines is one part of paste-up that gives newsletter editors a lot of trouble. Almost everyone agrees that it's a tedious and taxing job, but the professional results that are possible with transfer type make it well worth the effort.

Art-supply stores in many communities stock transfer type in scores of different sizes and faces. It's an inexpensive product that allows you to compose your own large-type headlines rather than relying on printers and typography houses, which are usually very costly.

Transfer type is packaged and sold in special wax-treated sheets. Each sheet contains several different copies of each letter of the alphabet, plus numerals and punctuation marks. To set a line of transfer type, you "transfer" the letters from this sheet one by one to another surface until you have spelled out a complete headline. It's a slow process, but transfer type can do wonders to dress up the pages of your newsletter. When reproduced, it looks just as professional as what you might get from your local typesetter.

Composing a headline with transfer type is simple, once you get the hang of it. The following six steps are involved. Each of these is illustrated on page 74.

1. Draw a straight line on a sheet of white paper with a nonreproducible blue pencil. This serves as a guideline for the line of type to make sure you keep it running straight and true.

2. Put the sheet of transfer type on the guideline with the appropriate letter in place. The wax on the back of the letters should be next to the paper, with the front of the letters facing toward you.

3. With a burnisher, a pencil, or some other pointed instrument, rub the letter until it sticks to the paper. Be sure to rub every part of the black letter thoroughly before lifting the transfer sheet.

4. Line up the next letter and rub it down in its proper position next to the first letter. Repeat this procedure until the headline is completed.

5. Place the white waxed sheet that comes with the transfer type over the entire headline. Rub the headline briskly through this sheet with a burnisher or a blunt object. This places a coat of wax over the headline to attach it permanently to the paper and protect it from dirt and grime.

6. Finally, cut out the headline and place it in its proper position on the layout sheet with other elements to form a newsletter page.

The most common problem that church newsletter editors have with transfer type is poor spacing and alignment (see illustration, p. 75). Notice the gap between l and t in the word *Fulton* in this newsletter. Be sure to put the letters within a word side by side so your readers will know they belong together. Don't leave breathing space like this between letters. And the best way to keep the line straight is to draw a guideline in nonreproducible blue pencil.

This example also shows why it's important to set your headlines on separate pieces of paper, then paste them down with all the other elements on the newsletter layout sheet. It's virtually impossible to get everything aligned when you're taking a wild guess about how much space the headline will fill.

Another common problem is using transfer type that is too large or too small for headlines (see illustration, p. 75). Notice that the type used for headlines in this newsletter doesn't seem to be quite as tall as the typewriter type which is used for body copy. It is bold and legible and set in all capitals, but it still doesn't give the contrast which makes for good headlines. If you use typewriter type for the body copy in your newsletter, the transfer type headlines should be at least 18 point and 24 point in size. The headline from this newsletter is 12-point type.

If you publish your newsletter frequently or have a lot of headlines to set, you might investigate the possibility of buying a headline-setting machine for your church office. These machines cost several hundred dollars, but they are easy to operate and they produce quality headlines quickly through a self-contained photographic process. The headline comes from the machine on reproduction-quality paper (see illustration, p. 75), ready to be trimmed and pasted down on the newsletter layout sheet. If you're interested, check with firms that sell copying machines and graphic arts supplies.

This covers the basics of paste-up and stencil preparation. But so far we have totally ignored the important question of how to use photographs in a church newsletter. Move on to the next chapter for some helpful pointers on this subject.

A Stylus with Letterguides

Stencil Scope Board

Tracing a Headline with a Stylus and a Letterguide

EVENING WORSHIP

7:15 p.m.

WAS IT YOU who devoted some week time to a Bible study and watched God bless some lives?

Three Different Styles of Type from the Same Typewriter

T U B I N G   D O W N   T H E   H I W A S S E E   R I V E R

Saturday, June 13, will be a new experience for many. 7th-12th graders will pack lunches and leave church at 8:30 a.m. to go tubing. The place we put in will supply tubes for us.

B A C K Y A R D   B I B L E   S T U D I E S -- Aug. 17 - 21

A Bible study time for our own young people at different homes each night with a time of recreation following will be the events of our backyard Bible studies.

 Youth Ministry

TOMMY PUCKETT
Minister to Youth

JUNIOR HIGH AFTERGLOW Sunday, June 7, for Putt-Putt tournament on Brainerd Road. The van will be taken.

YOUTH WORKING WITH CHILDREN'S ACTIVITIES PROGRAM training session will be on Saturday, June 6, from 10:00 a.m. until noon. You need to be here for instructions   and walking through the activities that are planned.

Typewriter Headlines Underlined, Capitalized, and Letter-spaced for Better Contrast

---

```
********************************************
*
*     IN MEMORIAM--JOHN  H.  BOTBYL
*
*         This is a difficult memoriam to write.
*     My dad did not attend Bethany Church regu-
*     larly, he was not a member of the Men's
*     Bible Class, nor did he participate in
*     any church social activity.
*         Maybe he was an introvert, as he
*     called himself, because he was orphaned
*     at 8 years of age and "traded" from one
*     unwanted situation to another, or it
*     could have been an undetected heart
*     problem diagnosed as nerves that plagued
*     him from his early thirties.
*         Whatever the reason, I would like to
*     ask for Christian love and understanding
*     for people who are not comfortable in
*     crowds--who do not want to associate--
*     who are different.
*         Accept them for what they are.  I
*     accepted my dad as an honest, respectable,
*     considerate, prudent individual and father.
*     To have changed him, I might have missed
*     his unassuming nature, his interesting
*     conversation, and his free and easy
*     counsel.
*
*                    --Richard H. Botbyl
*
********************************************
```

Copy Boxed with the Typewriter Asterisk (*) Key

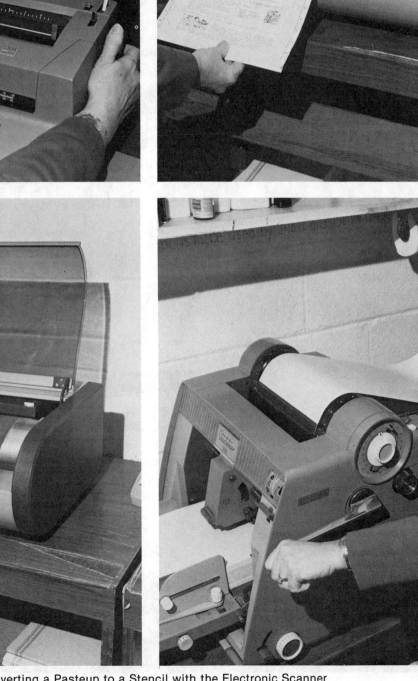

Converting a Pasteup to a Stencil with the Electronic Scanner

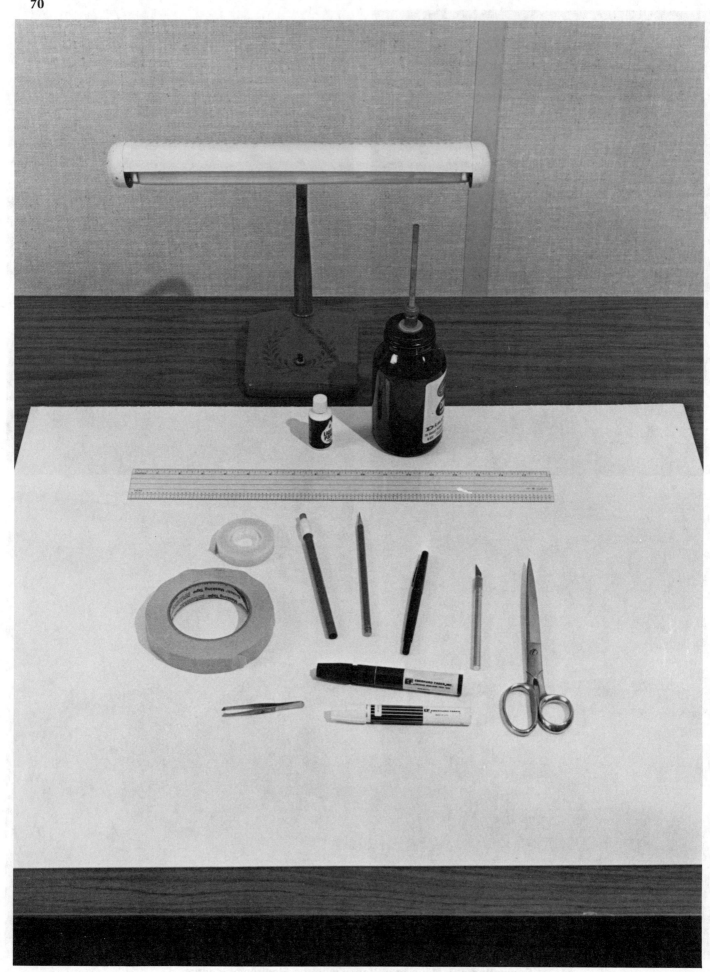

Basic Tools Needed for Paste - up Work

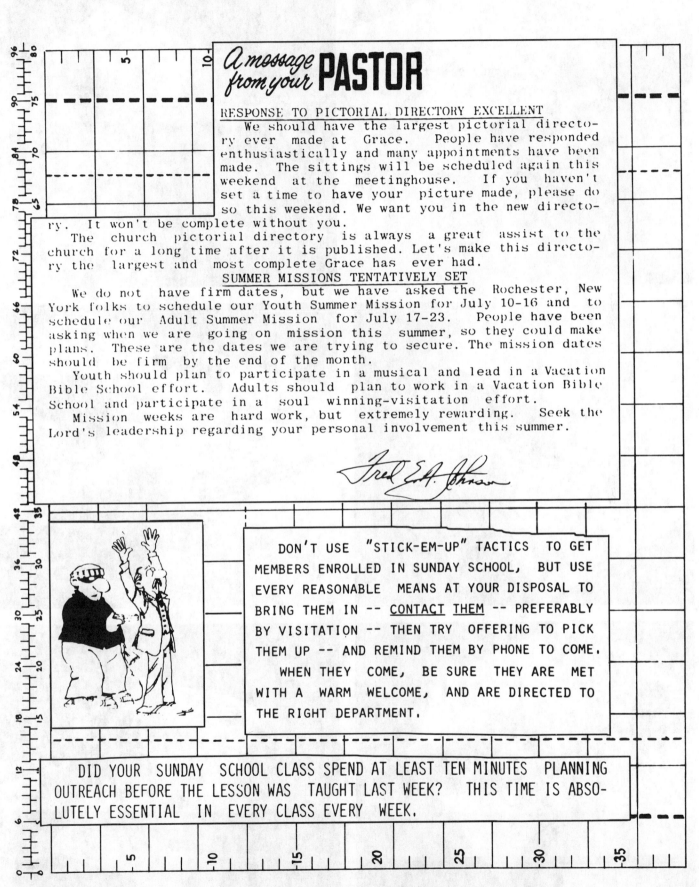

A message from your PASTOR

RESPONSE TO PICTORIAL DIRECTORY EXCELLENT

We should have the largest pictorial directory ever made at Grace. People have responded enthusiastically and many appointments have been made. The sittings will be scheduled again this weekend at the meetinghouse. If you haven't set a time to have your picture made, please do so this weekend. We want you in the new directory. It won't be complete without you.

The church pictorial directory is always a great assist to the church for a long time after it is published. Let's make this directory the largest and most complete Grace has ever had.

SUMMER MISSIONS TENTATIVELY SET

We do not have firm dates, but we have asked the Rochester, New York folks to schedule our Youth Summer Mission for July 10-16 and to schedule our Adult Summer Mission for July 17-23. People have been asking when we are going on mission this summer, so they could make plans. These are the dates we are trying to secure. The mission dates should be firm by the end of the month.

Youth should plan to participate in a musical and lead in a Vacation Bible School effort. Adults should plan to work in a Vacation Bible School and participate in a soul winning-visitation effort.

Mission weeks are hard work, but extremely rewarding. Seek the Lord's leadership regarding your personal involvement this summer.

Fred E. A. Johnson

DON'T USE "STICK-EM-UP" TACTICS TO GET MEMBERS ENROLLED IN SUNDAY SCHOOL, BUT USE EVERY REASONABLE MEANS AT YOUR DISPOSAL TO BRING THEM IN -- <u>CONTACT</u> <u>THEM</u> -- PREFERABLY BY VISITATION -- THEN TRY OFFERING TO PICK THEM UP -- AND REMIND THEM BY PHONE TO COME.

WHEN THEY COME, BE SURE THEY ARE MET WITH A WARM WELCOME, AND ARE DIRECTED TO THE RIGHT DEPARTMENT.

DID YOUR SUNDAY SCHOOL CLASS SPEND AT LEAST TEN MINUTES PLANNING OUTREACH BEFORE THE LESSON WAS TAUGHT LAST WEEK? THIS TIME IS ABSOLUTELY ESSENTIAL IN EVERY CLASS EVERY WEEK.

Preprinted Paste-up Layout Sheet

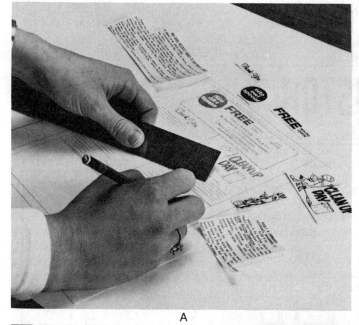

A

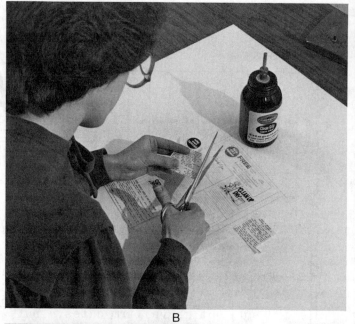

B

C

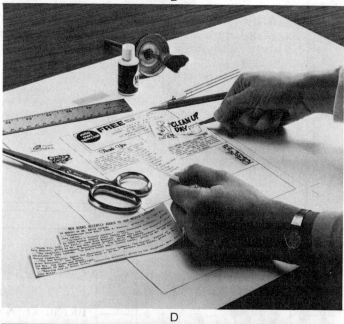

D

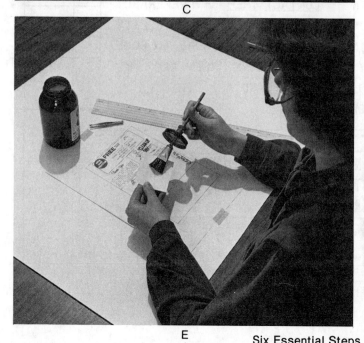

E

F

Six Essential Steps to Good Paste-ups

Singfest Begins

Monthly Singfest will begin Sun., Sept. 7, 9-9:15 a.m. Fourth grade and up invited!

College Address

If you will be attending school out-of-town (college, technical or business school, etc.) please give us your address as soon as possible

Putting a Neat Border Around a Block of Copy

Opportunities
FOR THE WEEK
of January 24-30

SUNDAY
9:40 a.m. . . . . Sunday School
11:00 a.m. . . . . . . Morning Worship
Cablecast Over Channel 10 Cablevision
Broadcast Over Radio Station WAZF
4:30 p.m. . . . . . Disciplelife Training
and Youth Choir
6:00 p.m. . . . . Church Training
7:00 p.m. . . . . Evening Worship
Broadcast Over Radio Station WAZF
Cablecast Over Channel 10 Cablevision
MONDAY
9:00 a.m. . . . . Church Staff Meeting
WEDNESDAY
7:00 a.m. . . Men's Prayer Breakfast
3:15 p.m. . . . . . . Music and Missions
Music Friends, Music Makers, Young
Musicians, Mission Friends, Girls in Action
5:30 p.m. . . . . . Family Night Supper
6:30 p.m. . . . . Mid-Week Service
6:30 p.m. . . . . . Royal Ambassadors
7:15 p.m. . . . . Sanctuary Choir

Opportunities
FOR THE WEEK
of January 24-30

SUNDAY
9:40 a.m. . . . . Sunday School
11:00 a.m. . . . . . . Morning Worship
Cablecast Over Channel 10 Cablevision
Broadcast Over Radio Station WAZF
4:30 p.m. . . . . . Disciplelife Training
and Youth Choir
6:00 p.m. . . . . Church Training
7:00 p.m. . . . . Evening Worship
Broadcast Over Radio Station WAZF
Cablecast Over Channel 10 Cablevision
MONDAY
9:00 a.m. . . . . Church Staff Meeting
WEDNESDAY
7:00 a.m. . . Men's Prayer Breakfast
3:15 p.m. . . . . . . Music and Missions
Music Friends, Music Makers, Young
Musicians, Mission Friends, Girls in Action
5:30 p.m. . . . . . Family Night Supper
6:30 p.m. . . . . Mid-Week Service
6:30 p.m. . . . . . Royal Ambassadors
7:15 p.m. . . . . Sanctuary Choir

Centering Lines of Type Inside a Box

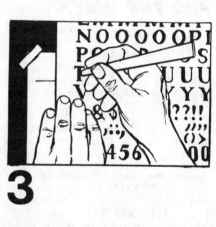

Dividing a Box into Equal Parts

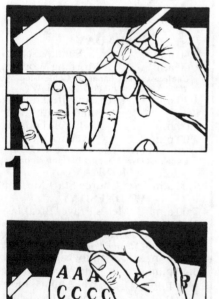
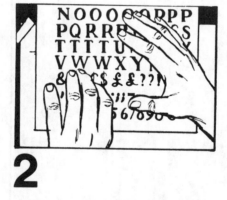

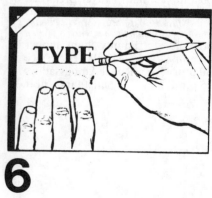

How to Compose a Transfer-Type Headline

ORDINATION

Fulton Hartzog

September 21   7:1

This Sunday marks another mile—
one of our sons. FULTON HARTZOG
Christian home. His parents, Way
ers and workers in our church. F
to full-time Christian service se
high school student at Farragut.
son-Newman College and Southweste
Texas, Fulton met and married th

To continue his active minist
ordained by his "home" church.
will convene at 2:30 p.m. this S
Hall. All ordained ministers an
attend.

Poor Spacing and Alignment of Transfer Type

VACATION BIBLE SCHOOL

VBS at Faith Lutheran will be held June
7-11 this summer. Please mark the dates
on your calendar. Note that it is a week
earlier this year. Watch future NEWS-
LETTERS and bulletins for opportunity
to sign-up to help teach or work in
other areas of VBS. Last year we had
37 teachers and aides and 170 children.
Can we exceed it this year?

==::==

Transfer Type Too Small for Good Headline Contrast

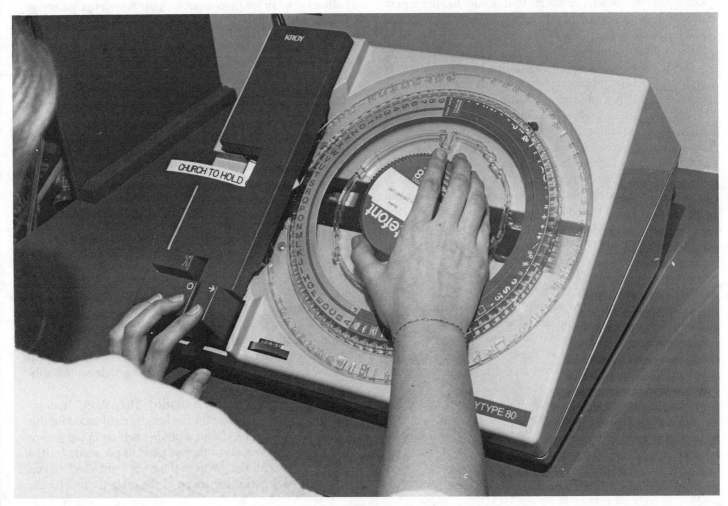

Setting Type on a Desk-Top Headline Machine

6
Using Photographs
In Your Newsletter

More and more churches are publishing photographs in their newsletters. But this is still one of those "iffy" situations for many congregations. You might consider it for your own church paper—*if* you are printing by a process that gives good reproduction of photos.

About Printing Processes

Offset printing is the one process that can guarantee quality reproduction of photographs with a minimum of effort. So if you're having your church paper printed by an outside printer, photos pose no problem. Your printer has the expensive equipment needed to reduce and enlarge photographs and break them down into the precise dot pattern they must have for flawless reproduction.

But if you're doing your own printing by mimeograph or copying machine, photographs are a different matter. It is possible to scan a photograph with an electronic stencil maker and get an image that reproduces quite well on a mimeograph machine. But every step in the production process has to be perfect before you can pull it off. The photograph must be a high-contrast, black-and-white print with a glossy surface. The scanner must be fine-tuned for precision reproduction. And the mimeograph machine has to be inked just right. If any of these variables aren't right on target, the photograph will probably come out looking faded and dim or, even worse, dark and shadowy. This same general principle also applies to reproducing photos by copying machine.

So, if you're printing by one of these processes, should you forget about publishing photos? Not just yet. There are a few things you can do to make it more feasible. First, talk with the technicians at the firm that sold you the printing equipment. They can show you how to wring every ounce of reproduction potential out of these machines. They could have some valuable tips on how to get a good image from photographs.

Another approach is to have your photographs turned into screened prints or halftone positives. This simple operation can be performed by an offset printer, a quick-print shop, or a photography studio. The printer simply rephotographs your black-and-white prints through a special screen that breaks the photos into a pattern of contrasting dots. Ask your printer for halftone positives—copies of these screened prints that you can paste down right on your newsletter page layout sheets.

These halftone positives will reproduce much better on an electronic stencil or a copying machine than your original photographs. To save money, have your printer make several of these screened prints at the same time.

Still another possibility is to invest in a screening kit for a Polaroid camera. This attachment automatically converts the instant photo that comes from the camera into a positive halftone, ready for placement on your newsletter paste-up. Check with a photography-supply store for complete details.

Photos and Their Possibilities

If photographs can be reproduced clearly in your newsletter, use them as liberally and as often as space and budget permit. In our visually oriented culture, readers appreciate the image of authority and timeliness which good photographs project. In addition to keeping the membership informed, they can also inspire, motivate, and entertain. Photography is being used aggressively and creatively in many church newsletters today (see illustrations, pp. 78-79). These examples may suggest some possibilities for your own church paper.

What better way to introduce a guest speaker to your membership than with a photograph? This satisfies the natural curiosity that all human beings have about strangers and gives the church some familiarity with the speaker before he arrives.

Good photographs are also effective for "know your church" features in the church newsletter. Photographs of the kindergarten ministry of one church added visual appeal as well as important information to the article on this subject.

Finally, the page of photos entitled "Holy Week" is an excellent technique for establishing just the right mood for this important week. The photographs focused on music groups and the church hostess as they worked to get ready for the Lenten season. All the events of the week were also listed on the page. And notice the shape of the cross formed by the white space around the four photos on the lower part of the page. The pictures and this symbolic arrangement helped to inspire a spirit of worship as the church approached this annual celebration.

Tips for Better Photographs

Now to the questions of composition and technique. How can you take better photographs for your church paper? What kind of photos reproduce best? The following tips should help you put the very best into the photos which you publish in your church newsletter.

1. For quality reproductions, use black-and-white photographs with a high-gloss finish. Color photos don't have the extreme contrast that is necessary for good publication photography: Sometimes you can get favorable reproductions from color prints, but generally they are a very poor substitute for black-and-white. And stay away from those dull, silky finishes that some studios and photo-finishing labs like to use on their prints. Photos with a high-gloss finish will reproduce much better.

2. The best photographs tell a story, make a statement, or express action. This means that if the pastor presents a plaque of appreciation to the church organist, it's always better to show the award being presented than to photograph them standing shoulder to shoulder looking at the camera. Never make the reader guess what's going on. He should be able to tell by looking at the picture.

3. When taking photographs of people, move in close until they fill almost the entire frame of the viewfinder on your camera. This eliminates details on either side that aren't an essential part of the shot.

4. Even if some unwanted side details show up in the finished print, these can be eliminated by a process known as cropping. To do this, place two L-shaped pieces of cardboard about two inches wide on the photo, then move these around until they frame out all the extraneous details. Mark the photo in the margins to show the printer where you want it cropped so these won't show up in print.

Take a look at the three illustrations on page 80 to see how the cropping process works. This technique can make a big difference in the visual impact of the photographs published in your newsletter.

5. Try to hold the number of people in a photograph to no more than four or five. This allows you to move in close for better action shots. When you're taking photos of an activity with a lot of people, such as a church banquet, photograph several small groups of a few people rather than trying to show the whole group in one shot.

6. If you absolutely must have a large-group shot, take a few minutes to get the people posed correctly before snapping the picture. If possible, group them into several rows of four or five persons each, right behind the other. This is much better than photographing them in a couple of rows that stretch all the way across the room. With this long-line approach, you have to move so far back to get everyone in the picture that no one is recognizable.

Take a close look at the photos from two church newsletters on page 81. They demonstrate both these methods of grouping people. See how much closer you can move in with your camera when the rows are just four or five people wide?

7. Finally, remember that even the best photographs accomplish little unless you tell the reader what's going on in the scenes. Look at the five photos on page 81, taken at the "Music and Missions Carnival" for one church. They were published in the church newsletter just as they appear here, without cutline or identifying copy of any kind. The only people who could appreciate these photos were church members who attended the event and who knew the people in the snapshots. Be sure to give your readers full information with every photo which you publish in the newsletter. Good pictures are always enriched by adequate identification copy.

So much for photographs and what they can do for your newsletter. Now let's examine the different printing processes to see which one is right for your church. This subject is covered in chapter 7.

WHAT YOU NEED TO KNOW ABOUT OUR. . .

KINDERGARTEN

Q. How long has First Baptist Church/Orlando had a Kindergarten program?

A. The Kindergarten program of First Baptist is beginning its 23rd year. We have taken every opportunity to build upon this excellent foundation toward an even better educational operation.

Q. What age child may attend?

A. Children, ages 2 through 5, may attend our school. The age group your child will be with is determined by his age on September 1.

Q. When do the classes meet?

A.
Class		Days
Kindergarten	(5 years)	M & F
Pre-Kindergarten	(4 years)	T-W-Th
	(4 years)	M & F
Developmental	(3 years)	T & Th
	(3 years)	M & F
	(2 years)	T & Th
	(2 years)	M & F

Classes meet from 8:30 to 12:00
Extended care is offered from 7:45 a.m. to 5:30 p.m.

Q. What should you look for in a preschool program?

A. If your child is one of the exceptional few who takes naturally to reading at an early age — you might be looking for a program that teaches him to read and write by the age of four.

Most authorities, however, would approve of a different kind of program — one that places reading and writing lower on the list of priorities for three and four year olds. They tell parents that a good program has these basic features:

It provides an additional warm setting for the child.

It provides a rich environment and varied learning expreiences.

It is staffed by caring, informed, and trained adults.

It provides a safe and attractive physical setting that promotes learning and healthy development.

Learning is tied to real life problems that require careful manipulation and free-wheeling experimentation.

SUPPLEMENT TO THE BEACON

Some Effective Uses of Photographs in Church Newsletters

HOLY WEEK

PALM SUNDAY
8:00 a.m. Worship Service
10:15 a.m.
Children's Choir
presenting
"The Singing Bishop"
by Hal H. Hopson
The story of the hymn:
ALL GLORY, LAUD AND
HONOR (#123 in Hymnal)
10:30 a.m.
Worship Service
Holy Communion at both
the
8:00 a.m. and 10:30
services

The music program is gearing up for the many events which are to take place during Passion Sunday and Holy Week. Kenneth Kroesche on the euphonium and Dick Morris at the organ, prepare the music for Good Friday Tenebrae Services. The Sanctuary Choir has put in many extra hours preparing the music for Passion Sunday and combined with the High School Choir, pictured here, will do the "Handel's Messiah" on Easter.

MAUNDY THURSDAY
7:00 p.m.
Pre-Service Concert
Mike Soukup-Classical
Guitar
Linda Galvan - Oboe
7:30 p.m.
Worship Service
Holy Communion
Meditation by
Rev. J. Linwood Kennedy

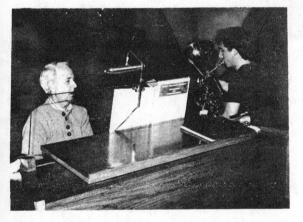

GOOD FRIDAY
9:00 a.m.
German Worship Service
Sermon by Rev. Richard Kuretsch
7:00 p.m.
Pre-Service Concert
Kenneth Kroesche, Euphonium
C. Richard Morris, Organist
The selections being performed are especially appropriate to the Good Friday mood. Program notes will be printed so that you may better understand the music.
7:30 p.m.
Tenebrae Service
"Service of Darkness"
by Dale Wood
The Sanctuary Choir
Meditation by
Rev. J. Linwood Kennedy

EASTER
6:30 a.m.
Sunrise Service
The reenactment of the resurrection events through Scripture, Tableau, and Hymns.
8:00 and 10:30 a.m.
Two Identical Services
Sermon by
Rev. J. Linwood Kennedy
Glorious music by te combined Sanctuary and Senior High Choirs, Organ and Brass Quartet including William Foster, Trumpet: Nancy Dornbusch, Trumpet; Kenneth Kroesche, Euphonium; and William Piece, Trombone.
The exciting "Hallelujah Chorus" by Handel will conclude each service. (Children are asked to bring cut flowers for the cross in the Sanctuary.).

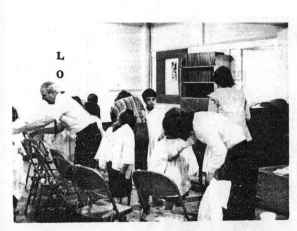

Susan Parsley, Jennifer Burtch and Donna McIntyre assist Dick Morris in fitting robes on members of the Children's Choir in preparation for "The Singing Bishop" to be presented Palm Sunday at 10:15 in the Sanctuary.

Helen Wahl, our resident food services co-ordinator, prepares one of the many delicious suppers during the Lenten season. Helen puts in many hours on Wednesdays during this time of the year since she not only prepares the suppers but also the food for the Wednesday Noon Luncheon that is a regular event throughout the year.

Crop Photographs to Leave Out Unnecessary Details

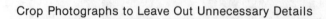

1. Photo Shot Close in but Published without Cropping

2. The Cropping Process

3. Same Photo After Close Cropping

IN RECENT MONTHS Fr. William McCarthy observed his 30th anniversary as a pri-
by the South Shore Chamber of Commerce "for his work with the underprivileged
Quincy." On such happy occasions Fr. McCarthy and members of his family have
moments at a family get-together. Joining with the Pastor on these occasions were (fro
Hector Perrone, sister; Melissa Perrone, grandniece; Christopher Perrone, gr
McCarthy; (standing from left) Hector Perrone, brother-in-law William Perrone,
Perrone, Mrs. John Perrone, and John Perrone, nephew.

Front Row (l to r) Dana Vickrey, Linda Tallman, Rhonda Dewbre,
Sidney Stockdale, Julie Baskin, Ruth Reeder, Alice Rushmore,
Clay Pickering, Donna Rivera, Steve Brewster, Becky Jo (Lindsey)
Timmons, Debbie Hurt, Ruth Crenshaw. Second Row (l to r) Linda
Blagg, Jim Blagg, Mike Peden, Nancy Williams, David Peterson,
Skeet Tingle, Emily Noel, Patrice Kelly, Steve Simons, Brenda
Parker, Kim Hoffman, Steve Hurt, Phil Crenshaw

Place Large Groups in Short Rows for Better Photos

MUSIC & MISSIONS CARNIVAL

Photos Published without Identifying Cutlines

7
Reproduction and Printing Ideas

Your church has probably already decided what printing process it will use to reproduce the newsletter—whether by mimeograph, offset, or photocopier. Like most congregations, yours has already invested in the equipment you need to get the job done. So why consider this subject at all? Because it's always helpful to have the facts in case you want to switch to another system in the future. Besides that, so many changes are taking place every year in the printing field that you should constantly evaluate your procedure to make sure you are using the best approach.

The best way to decide what printing procedure is right for your church is to ask yourself a series of questions. Following are some probing questions that should help you determine what approach is best and how to save money in newsletter production.

Should We Do Our Own Printing or Hire It Done?

The most basic question of all is whether to buy the equipment needed to do the printing at the church or whether to take the job to an outside printer. The interesting thing about this question is that a contract printing firm may be ideal for a very small church or a very large congregation. The reasons for this are simple. A small church may be issuing such a limited number of newsletters that it's not economically feasible to buy and maintain its own printing equipment. And a large church may be issuing the newsletter in such big quantities that an outside printing firm can do the job on its high-speed presses at a better price.

If your church is small—300 members or less—and you issue your newsletter twice a month or monthly, consider having it reproduced by a nearby quick-print shop or local printer. At least, ask them to give you price quotes so you can compare their figures with the cost of printing it yourself on your own equipment. You might be pleasantly surprised with their prices. And remember that quick-printers use offset presses; these will yield a much more professional reproduction than your own mimeograph equipment.

Likewise, if your church is large—say in the 2,000-member category—check into the possibility of outside printing for your newsletter. And remember that the cost of paper becomes a major consideration with high press runs

and frequent publication. Some larger churches have even moved to a tabloid newspaper format for their newsletters for that very reason. Paper costs have shot up dramatically in recent years, and specialty tabloid printers have sprung up all over the country to offer this option to interested distributors of publications. You might check with one of these specialty printers in your area to see if the tabloid format offers any cost savings for your church.

As you think about an outside printer vs. doing it yourself, don't forget that scheduling is also an important consideration. If you publish weekly, for example, you might find it better to do your own printing, even though an outside printer could do the job for less money. If he should print the newsletter, can he get it back to you on schedule week after week to enable you to meet your mailing deadlines? As a busy church secretary or editor, you may not have the time to be running back and forth to the local print shop. Doing your own printing may be your only choice if you are on a tight schedule.

What Printing Process Is Best for Us?

Once you have decided to do your own printing, you face the question of which process is best for your situation. It depends on many factors, including the number of copies printed for each issue of the newsletter, cost, speed, convenience, and ease of operation.

Thirty years ago the choice was simple. Practically every church newsletter printed in the church office was done by mimeograph. And even today, with the advent of the electronic stencil, mimeograph is still going strong in many churches. The beauty of this system is that it's fast and low in cost, the paper is inexpensive, and it's easy to operate. Any church office worker can operate a mimeograph machine after just a few minutes of elementary instruction. But working with the messy ink on one of these machines is a real problem. Most church secretaries have learned not to wear their best clothes to work on mimeographing day!

One challenger to the faithful mimeograph machine is the desk-top offset duplicator. This machine is similar to a mimeograph in size and about as easy to operate. It is also fast. But one problem is the cost. It generally costs about two or three times more than a mimeograph. In addition, the offset duplicator requires an expensive backup platemaking machine before you can capitalize on any of its advantages, which includes the reproduction of photographs. And unlike the mimeograph machine, the offset duplicator requires a thorough cleaning after every use. This brings us right back to the problem of messiness, which many church office workers find objectionable.

An offset duplicator may be a good choice for your newsletter, if you can justify its higher cost by doing other types of printing for the church, such as envelopes and letterheads. But remember that quality printing like this requires someone who will develop the skills that are necessary for professional results. If you don't have someone like this on the church staff, you will probably never capitalize on the advantages of owning your own offset equipment.

The Copying Machine Trend

The reproduction tool that is rapidly replacing the mimeograph machine as the preferred printing method is the photocopying machine. For years copying machines were too slow and expensive to be taken seriously as a newsletter printing contender around most church offices.

But all that changed as technology pushed the prices of office copiers lower and lower, while the printing speed climbed higher and higher. The modern church office of today is just as likely to be using an office copier as a mimeograph machine to print the newsletter. And more and more church offices will switch to the copying machine in the years ahead as the trend continues.

The copying machine combines simplicity, cleanliness, and ease of operation in one convenient operation that seems to be ideal for church newsletter reproduction. The efficient dry copiers of today have eliminated the messy fluids and toners that were an essential part of photocopying just a few years ago. The sleek, modern models can do everything from printing on both sides of the sheet, to reducing and enlarging the master, to collating the job after it's finished.

Here are some guidelines to keep in mind if you are shopping around for an office copier to produce your newsletter and other church printing jobs. Even if you already have a copier, you will be shopping for a replacement model some day, so these guidelines should still be helpful.

1. Begin by assessing your needs. How many copies per month are you likely to be producing? What will you use the copier for besides the newsletter? This will automatically help you to focus your shopping efforts on those models from several different manufacturers which are designed to handle your monthly copying volume. For your convenience, the names and addresses of many copying machine manufacturers are published on page 108 of this book. Write them for literature about their products so you can begin to narrow the copier possibilities down to a manageable list.

2. Office copiers can be divided for convenience into several distinct categories to help you focus more precisely on what you need: (1) small desk-top models with few special features that make about 10 to 20 copies per minute, (2) larger models with features such as copy reduction and enlargement that make about 20 to 40 copies per minute, and (3) even larger, faster, and more specialized models that make from 40 to 50 or more copies per minute.

3. From this wide range of copiers available, you should be able to find one that is ideal for your printing needs. Smaller churches may be able to manage with one of the small, inexpensive models. Mid-range copiers in category 2 above are generally adequate for churches that make 4,000 to 5,000 copies per month. And a heavy-duty commercial model may be needed in a large church with a weekly newsletter that circulates 2,000 or more copies per issue. Make sure you buy a copier that is adequate for your needs. As many church secretaries can testify, trying to squeeze out more copies than the machine is capable of will lead to frustrating delays and expensive breakdowns.

4. Remember that one of the quirks of an office copier is its need for regular servicing. It must be cleaned regularly to keep the reproduction sharp and clear. And even with the best of preventive maintenance, it will still break down at the very time when you need it most. If you do switch to a photocopier for newsletter production, you might hang on to your old mimeograph equipment, just in case. It might come in handy as a backup system if the copier should quit right in the middle of a pressing deadline.

How Can We Save Money on Paper?

No matter what system of reproduction you use for the newsletter, they all have a way of gobbling up monstrous amounts of paper. It's no secret that the biggest expense of production for most churches is the paper cost. How to save money on this commodity is an important question for every church paper editor. The following tips should help you in this phase of the production process.

1. *Use standard-size sheets that produce no paper waste.* Did you ever wonder how an odd size like 8½x11″ came to be accepted as the standard for typing paper, mimeo bond, letterheads, and newsletter pages? It's because the paper from which these items are cut comes from the mill in 17x22″ sheets. Four pieces of 8½x11″ paper can be cut from this larger sheet without any waste. Other standard sheet sizes produced by paper mills include 23x35″, 25x38″, 35x45″, and 38x50″. Make sure your newsletter is a size that can be cut from one of these larger sheets with a minimum of waste (see illustration on p. 86). This is the all-important first step that results in a cost savings on the paper stock for your church publication.

2. *Plan efficiently for maximum savings.* Occasionally a church newsletter is published with one or two blank pages at the end. You don't have to be an economist to figure out that this is a big waste of the church's resources. Two blank pages times a total circulation of 450 equals 900 squandered pages! With better planning, the newsletter editor could have expanded the issue to fill all the available space or cut the copy by a page or two to eliminate the blank pages.

Careful planning like this can help you hold your paper costs in line.

3. *Experiment with different weights and types of paper*. The cost of paper varies considerably, depending on its texture, weight, and type. For example, mimeo paper is low in cost compared to other types because it's made of coarse materials that are designed to absorb the ink. But mimeo paper is available in different weights. Why use a 24-pound paper when a less-expensive 20-pound weight might give the same results? The only way you'll know for sure is to experiment with these two weights. If you can get by with the lighter weight, the savings in paper cost might be considerable across the period of a year.

Visit your local paper supplier, and tell him what printing process you are using. Ask him to explain the difference between the various weights and types of paper that are designed for your printing system. A little investigation at this point could save your church some real money on its paper bill.

4. *Buy in bulk quantities*. Another way to save money on paper is to buy it in huge lots. Check with your paper supplier to see what quantities offer the best buy. If a neighboring church uses the same paper stock, you might even lump your order together for greater savings and split the shipment after it's delivered. Paper is not difficult to store; it doesn't deteriorate; and you know you will use it eventually. So why not order in the quantities that can bring you the very best price?

So much for reproduction systems and how to save money on paper. What about mailing the newsletter? How can you get this job done quickly and conveniently?

Move on to the next chapter for some answers to these questions.

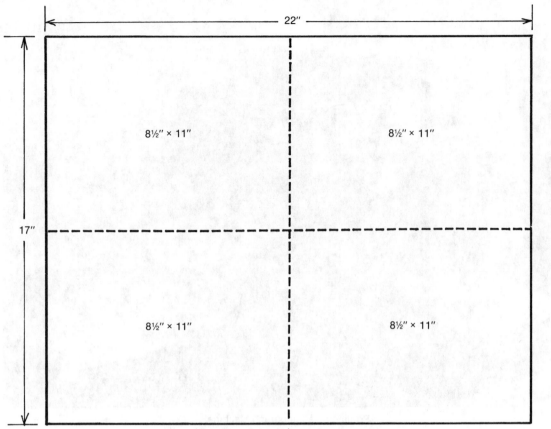

Four Sheets of 8½″ × 11″ Paper Cut
From One 17 × 22″ Sheet, with No Waste

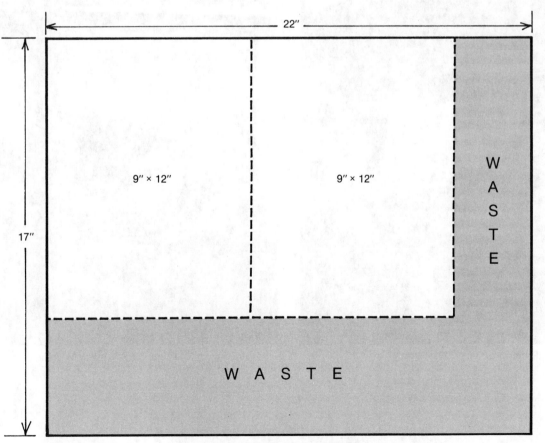

Two Sheets of 9 × 12″ Paper Cut from the same
17 × 22″ Sheet, Resulting in Significant Waste

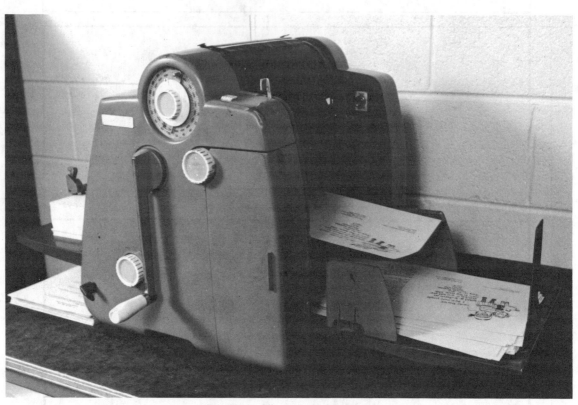

Printing by Mimeograph Machine

Printing by Small Offset Press

Printing by Copying Machine

8
Circulation and Mailing Suggestions

At first glance, the questions of circulation and mailing don't seem to be such a big deal for most church newsletter editors. "We send the paper to all our members and let it go at that" is a typical approach to the subject. But what about inactive and nonresident members? How long do you continue to send the newsletter to faithful members after they have moved away and joined other churches? Can the newsletter be used to reach prospective members? These questions prove that the subject deserves serious consideration. Why go to the trouble of publishing a newsletter at all unless you plan to make it as useful as possible to the church?

Let's explore this question from two different perspectives—(1) who should receive the church newsletter, and (2) how to mail it.

Recipients of the Newsletter

For best results, a church should have a consistent and orderly approach to the question of who receives the newsletter. To develop your own philosophy, look over the following list of suggested recipients.

Church members. The primary audience for the newsletter, of course, consists of church members. Make sure that new members are added to the mailing list as soon as they join the church. And work just as hard to keep the list updated as members move to new locations within the community and experience changes in their family status. Be particularly aware of changes that may be necessary because of deaths or divorces within the membership. For example, the newsletter should not continue to be addressed to "Mr. and Mrs. John Doe" long after the death of one of these members.

In some congregations, members move frequently within the neighborhood served by the church. To stay on top of these changes, you might publish a change-of-address notice frequently in the newsletter (see illustration, p. 90). Encourage your members to tell you in advance when they plan to move. This way, you avoid charges for address changes returned by the post office.

All churches would agree that active members who live nearby should receive the newsletter. But what about resident members who seldom attend? Before you strike them

off the mailing list, remember that the newsletter may be their only contact with the church. They should continue to receive this regular reminder of the church's concern as long as they are members, no matter what their pattern of support.

The one exception to this rule is if they specifically request to have their names removed. This does happen occasionally if members develop a negative attitude toward the church and quit attending for that reason.

While you're thinking about different types of church members, don't forget those who are temporarily away but who are still an essential part of your church family. This category includes college students, people in the military service, those on temporary job assignments overseas or in other states, and older members who are spending the winter in warmer climates. These people need to stay informed about their church. And what better way for the congregation to stay in touch than by sending the newsletter regularly while they are away?

Finally, what to do about all those members who are classified as nonresident? Most congregations have scores of these on the church roll—members who may have been active and involved for a while. But now they have moved all the way across town or out of state without transferring their memberships to other churches. Technically, they are still members of your church, but they contribute nothing toward its support. Should these members continue to receive the newsletter?

One logical answer to this problem is to place these people in a special nonresident category on the church newsletter mailing list. Send them a copy of the paper in a special mailing two or three times per year. This could be just the reminder that some of them need to take their membership seriously and affiliate with other congregations.

Former members. Former members of the church constitute another category of possible newsletter recipients. Active members who move away and immediately join other churches often ask to receive the newsletter, just to keep up with the congregation that was an important part of their lives for many years. It would be cold and unfeeling to deny these requests, but you also have to be careful that they don't get out of hand. Names like these that you keep on the list across a period of years can add considerably to the production costs.

One good way to deal with this problem is to give the address plates for former members a special code. This code should include the dates when they started receiving the church paper as former members. After they have received the newsletter for a year or so, send them a request card which they must mail back in order to keep their names on the mailing list. Many former members will let the newsletter drop as soon as they get adjusted to their new church home.

Prospective members. Forward-looking churches are also discovering that the church paper can be used to cultivate prospects and enlist new members. Names of prospects are gathered in many ways—through the Sunday School, from visitors' cards in worship services, through visitation in the community, and from church members themselves, who provide names of neighbors, friends, relatives, and business associates.

As soon as you receive names of bonafide prospects, prepare pressure-sensitive labels for a special mailing of the newsletter. The first copy might be enclosed with a letter from the minister about the church and its ministries. Explain that the paper reflects the inner life of an active and caring congregation. Then let the newsletter serve as a "silent salesman" for your church as you mail copies of the next three or four issues. This technique is particularly good with prospects who are "shopping around" at several different churches before making up their minds which one to join. The paper can serve as a continuing reminder of your church's concern.

Local businesses and publications. In addition to informing members, former members, and prospective members of your church, the newsletter can also serve as a valuable public relations ally for your congregation. A local real estate agency, for example, could use the church paper to show clients that an active church is located in the neighborhood where they plan to relocate.

And what about the community bank or branch bank that holds the mortgage on your church property? Don't forget influential political leaders, such as the mayor and local and district representatives. These are people who need to stay informed about your church and its constructive work in the community. What better way to keep them informed than through the pages of your newsletter? Place them on the mailing list so they will receive it regularly.

Another possible recipient who deserves special mention is the religion editor of the local newspaper. If this person receives your newsletter, he may see occasional articles that he would like to expand into a feature, resulting in some valuable free publicity for your church. Make sure this person and other appropriate representatives of the local media are on your mailing list.

Newsletter exchange. Finally, place several other churches on your mailing list in exchange for receiving their newsletters regularly. This is a great way to pick up fresh ideas for your own church paper. Include churches of other denominations as well as those of like faith in this exchange agreement. This gives you a broader range of ideas from which to choose.

To keep your newsletter exchange from getting out of hand, conduct a thorough purging of this system every couple of years. Mail everyone with whom you are swapping church papers a special card that must be returned if they are to stay on the list. This will remove most of those who have lost interest in your publication.

This covers the question of who should receive your church paper. Now let's consider some pointers on how to mail your newsletter efficiently and inexpensively.

Newsletter Mailing Pointers

When it comes to mailing the newsletter, it's dangerous to give specific how-to-do-it instructions. So much depends on how many copies you mail and how your local post office interprets the guidelines that apply to bulk mail. Nevertheless, there are a few general principles that should help you in this important part of the job.

Use the system that fits your circulation needs. Some churches mail thousands of copies of the newsletter every issue, while others send out only a few hundred. Obviously, congregations at these two extremes will need different mailing systems to get the job done.

Many high-circulation churches have moved to computerization of their mailing lists. All changes to the list are entered on a central data bank. Then the computer prints out the list on pressure-sensitive labels, all neatly arranged in zip code sequence. Finally, the labels are applied with sophisticated mailing equipment. The high speed provided by modern equipment is essential if a high-circulation newsletter is to be mailed on time. This is a good example of the principle of using the mailing system that fits a church's circulation needs.

This approach to mailing the newsletter makes particularly good sense if your church has a computer and you have already computerized many other tasks in your church office, such as bookkeeping and membership records management. The computer software you are using may have a feature that allows you to print out your newsletter mailing list on special one-up pressure-sensitive label stock. (See pp. 107-108 of this book for a list of computer software systems for churches as well as manufacturers of automatic label-applying machines.)

Check the illustrations on page 91 to see what a computer-generated one-up mailing list on pressure-sensitive labels looks like. Also pictured on page 91 is an automatic mailing machine that can apply these mailing labels to your church newsletter at the rate of about 5,000 per hour.

But some churches that mail only a few hundred copies of the newsletter can get by without investing in any expensive mailing equipment. It's possible with a system known as the "poor man's mailing list." You simply type your mailing list in the three-column format required for reproduction on a sheet of pressure-sensitive label stock, 8½x11″ in size. Then you use your office copying machine or the copier at a quick-print shop to reproduce the master list on this sheet of labels. This simple procedure yields instant pressure-sensitive address labels, 33 per sheet, ready to peel off and stick down on the copies of your church newsletter (see illustration, p. 90).

Between this "poor man's mailing list" and computerized mailing, there are dozens of other systems for churches, including addressing machines that use metal, plastic, or paper plates. Your local mailing-accessories dealer can help you design a system that is in line with your church's budget and the circulation of your newsletter.

Use the most cost-effective permit. No matter what particular mailing system you use, you will probably mail the church paper under a special bulk rate made available by the Postal Service to churches and other nonprofit organizations. Bulk mail of this type may be mailed under a second-class or a third-class permit.

In most cases, the second-class rate is cheaper, since you pay by the number of pounds mailed rather than by the number of pieces in the mailing. Check with the postmaster at your local post office to see if your newsletter qualifies for the second-class rate. It depends on the process you use to print your newsletter. And postmasters in various parts of the country have been known to interpret the postal regulations differently. The best approach is to check with local postal officials and follow their guidance and advice.

Use volunteer help. Addressing and sorting each issue of the newsletter for mailing is an ideal task for volunteer workers, particularly retired persons and senior adults. They may be looking for constructive ways to spend their time and help their church at the same time. Why not enlist them to help in this important ministry? It could free up your time for more creative pursuits, like planning some unusual features for the next issue of the church paper.

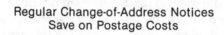

MOVING?

Please print your new address and phone number and drop the completed form into the offering plate or mail to the church.

Name _____

Address _____

City _____ State _____ Zip _____

Phone Number _____

Regular Change-of-Address Notices
Save on Postage Costs

Mailing List Copied on Pressure-Sensitive Label Stock

Mrs. Mary Chrisman 3174 Brookview Drive Anytown, NJ 17610	Mr. & Mrs. Jodi Barnes 231 Greentree Drive Anytown, NJ 17611	Mr. Harvey Kellogg 1513 Blue Bell Street Anytown, NJ 17611
Mr. and Mrs. C. W. Coffer 310 Hoffman Road Anytown, NJ 17610	Dr. Joseph D. Battle 196 Delvin Drive Anytown, NJ 17611	Joseph D. Blackwell 213 Holdenfield Anytown, NJ 17612
Mrs. Roger Cole 517 Nell Parkway Anytown, NJ 17610	The Thomas Curry Family 280 Knight Road Anytown, NJ 17611	Earle and Penny Crawf 213 Nichols Street Anytown, NJ 17612
Terry Coleman 4197 Darlington Road Anytown, NJ 17610	Samuel and Elaine Curtis 659 Farrah Court Anytown, NJ 17611	Miss Josephine DeBer 65 Crutchfield Circl Anytown, NJ 17612
Darlene and Roger Cook 114 New Braunfels Pike Anytown, NJ 17610	Miss Ginny Daley 231 Richfield Terrace Anytown, NJ 17611	Mr. Bobby Dennis 106 West Valley Lan Anytime, NJ 17612
Mrs. Irene Coreen 4912 Jonquil Circle Anytown, NJ 17610	Joe and Debbie Darden 461 Kathy Jo Circle Anytown, NJ 17611	Mr. and Mrs. Richar 234 Sherry Way Anytown, NJ 17612
Mrs. Pam Crawford 5107 Glasstech Place Anytown, NJ 17610	Mr. & Mrs. Harold Davis 1352 Roland Place Anytown, NJ 17611	Miss Emogene Dosse 867 Laguardian Pla Anytown, NJ 17612

Mrs. Irene Estelle Coreen
4912 Jonquil Circle
Anytown, NJ 17610

Mr. Earle T. Crawford
213 Nichols St.
Anytown, NJ 17610

Mrs. Mary Crisman
3174 Brookview Dr.
Anytown, NJ 17610

Mr. Joseph D. Blackwell
213 Holdenfield
Anytown, NJ 17611

Joe and Debbie Darden
461 Kathy Jo Circle
Anytown, NJ 17614

Miss Jodi M. Spielberg
ld Terrace

Computer-Generated Newsletter Mailing List
on One-Up Pressure-Sensitive Labels

Applying Labels with a High-Speed Labeling Machine

9
Using the Computer
in Newsletter Production

More and more congregations are discovering what a wonderful tool the computer is around the church office. With the right software and an attached printer, a computer can keep records of the members' financial contributions, do bookkeeping and checkwriting chores, maintain an up-to-date membership file, print out these files for an annual membership directory, record and analyze attendance by individual members, maintain a master list of church organizations and the people who participate in these activities, and keep a running inventory of church supplies.

The computer is also a useful tool when it comes to production of the newsletter and other church publications, such as the weekly worship bulletin and promotional brochures and flyers. Word processing, mailing list production, and desk-top publishing are three functions of the computer that are especially helpful in newsletter production work.

Word Processing

Using a computer to produce the copy for your church newsletter makes a lot of sense, even if you have to print the copy out and paste it up article by article to create your page layouts. Making corrections in a document that has been word processed by computer is a snap. You simply save the documents on a hard disk or a floppy disk and make changes electronically until you have it exactly like you want it before the final printout.

This is also a great feature when you discover that an article is too long or too short to fill an allotted space. It's easy to cut or add words or change the original document until it's just the length you need. A computer, with its word-processing capabilities, eliminates the time-consuming process of retyping these complete articles to make them fit your newsletter page.

Most integrated church management software systems (see list of suppliers on p. 107) include a word-processing program as part of the total software package. In addition to writing letters and reports with word processing, use this capability of your computer system to streamline the process of producing copy for your newsletter. For best results, you will need a printer that produces a clear, near-letter-quality impression. These results are possible today on many high-speed dot-matrix printers as well as the slower daisy-wheel printers.

Mailing List Production

Another time-consuming task handled efficiently by a computer is the maintenance of the church newsletter mailing list. This task is frustrating because of the constant changes required to keep a mailing list up to date and sorted in zip code sequence to meet postal regulations. But once a mailing list is computerized, names and addresses can be changed electronically in a fraction of the time required for a manual system.

Many integrated church management software systems (see list of suppliers on p. 107) include a mailing list maintenance program as part of the total software package. Individual, stand-alone mailing list programs can also be purchased from mail order firms or retail software stores at reasonable prices.

These programs allow you to customize and set up your mailing list to your requirements, then print it out in different formats on pressure-sensitive labels for quick-and-easy application to your newsletter for mailing. (See chapter 8, pp. 87-91, and the list of suppliers on p. 108 for information on automatic label-applying equipment.)

Desk-Top Publishing

"Desk-top publishing" are two of the latest buzz words among computer users. They are even being heard around church offices as secretaries and other staff members discuss the latest technology that promises to take some of the hassle out of publishing the newsletter.

This phrase refers to the system by which all the publishing tasks normally performed by specialized graphic-arts experts are done on computer. These tasks include keyboarding the manuscript, typesetting, arranging the elements into a page design, and outputting a finished, camera-ready master ready to print. Because the hardware for performing all these specialized tasks—a personal computer and a laser printer—will fit on top of a desk, this system is referred to as "desk-top publishing."

The breakthrough that made desk-top publishing possible was the development of the laser printer. These highly sophisticated electronic instruments are capable of printing a document at high speed in a resolution pattern that approaches the quality obtained from a commercial typesetting machine. Even the best dot-matrix printers, by contrast, have a very coarse resolution printing pattern that outputs documents far below the typeset-quality look of a laser.

In addition to a laser printer, desk-top publishing also requires special software to drive the system. Most desk-top publishing software packages (see list of suppliers on p. 108) have everything you need, including several different sizes and styles of type, stock layout forms, and utility programs, to output typeset, camera-ready pages for your newsletter. However, make sure you investigate a specific software package thoroughly before you buy. Some of this software is easier to use than others. And some packages are designed for computers with specific operating systems. Make sure the software is compatible with your computer as well as your laser printer.

Some marketers of church management software systems are packaging these desk-top publishing programs with their systems. For example, PageMaker software by the Aldus Corporation is offered by the Church Information System (CIS; see illustration on p. 95). Keep in mind that purchasing desk-top publishing software as part of a package deal is generally less expensive than buying it as a separate item.

The third element of a desk-top publishing system is the computer—the central processing unit itself. Because of the complexity of desk-top publishing software, you will need a computer with at least 640 kilobytes of memory. And a 20-megabyte hard disk is also a necessity to accommodate the fonts of type and utility programs that come with most desk-top publishing software. Other computer enhancements frequently needed are a graphics card installed in the computer and an oversize monitor to allow you to view a full page of text.

Before buying a specific software, be sure to ask about its computer requirements. These are generally spelled out in brochures about their products available directly from the software manufacturers (see list of suppliers on p. 108).

Some Precautions and Guidelines

Perhaps desk-top publishing sounds like a good way to simplify newsletter production in your church. But before you plunge in, do some hard-headed thinking about costs, complexity of the system, and your own expectations.

Take your time. Don't become so excited about getting into desk-top publishing that you buy the first system you see and then start using it without so much as reading the instructions! Take a slow, deliberate approach in your shopping and implementation.

If you try to computerize your church's record-keeping and start desk-top publishing at the same time, you may be biting off more than you and the rest of the church can handle at one time. Remember that people can tolerate only so much change. Even if you buy your church management software and desk-top publishing software at the same time, gauge carefully whether all these changes should be implemented together. You may be better off to tackle them one at a time.

Consider the expense. Remember that desk-top publishing is a costly move which requires a laser printer, special software, and perhaps the upgrading of your present computer. To hold these expenses in line, consider buying the software so you can format the pages of your newsletter in your church office.

But you can avoid the expense of a laser printer by having the pages printed out by a quick-print shop or computer store in your city that offers this service. This approach will allow you to spread the cost of getting into desk-top publishing across a period of two or three years. After you perfect the technique of formatting your newsletter pages and decide you want to stay with this system permanently, then you could buy your own laser printer.

Don't expect too much. Before you invest in a desk-top publishing system for your church, think carefully about what it will and will not do. This new production process will save church staff time and maybe even save the church money over a period of several years. But it *will not* automatically produce a better-designed church newsletter or fill the publication with sparkling content. As always, these things depend on the time, creativity, and painstaking effort of the person responsible for producing the newsletter issue after issue.

To get this point well in mind, take a look at the front pages of two different church newsletters that were produced by desk-top publishing (see illustrations, p. 95). Both these publications were typeset and paginated with desk-top publishing software, then printed out on a laser printer. One is dull and unimaginative; it seems to depend on large type to shout its message to the reader. But the other is much more visually exciting. The difference is not in the software but in the care and creativity with which these two pages were designed.

Work, train, and learn. The two examples discussed above lead naturally into another important guideline about desk-top publishing: Don't buy a computer-based publishing system until you are willing to work, train, and learn in order to get professional results. Consider subscribing to a desk-top publishing newsletter or magazine (see list of publications on p. 106) for helpful tips from graphic experts on layout and design.

Learn from others. Finally, talk to other church newsletter editors who have already started desk-top publishing about their experience with this new technology. Find out what hardware and software they are using and whether they would recommend these to others. What mistakes did they make that you might be able to avoid? What parts of their publishing operation were the most difficult to convert to an electronic system? How long did they work with the software until they could produce an acceptable camera-ready page? Did they get adequate technical support and answers to their questions from the manufacturer of the software system which they bought? Getting answers to questions like these should help immeasurably as you select a system for your own church and launch your own program of electronic publishing.

One actual church newsletter analyzed in this book (see Case Study #5, pp. 98-99) is produced by a desk-top publishing system. Be sure to read this case study carefully for additional insights into this fascinating publishing technology as it relates to the production of the church newsletter.

95

Unimaginative Computer-Produced
Front Page

A More Creative Computer-Produced
Front Page

PageMaker Desktop Publishing Software on a Church Information System (CIS) Computer

A Newsletter Page, Formatted by CIS's PageMaker Software,
As It Appears on the Computer Screen

The Same Newsletter Page Printed Out on a Laser Printer

10
Five Outstanding Newsletters and What Makes Them Tick

Every phase of newsletter production has been discussed in chapters 1—9 of this book. We have examined all the essentials of a first-class church paper: a frequency and format geared to the unique needs of the church, good content, attractive layout and design, careful attention to details in paste-up and stencil preparation, tasteful and creative use of photographs, and quality reproduction.

Now that we have established the groundwork, let's do a detailed analysis of five different church newsletters. This analysis should show how these churches are mixing all these elements of production together to produce outstanding parish papers. These congregations have been selected not only because they are doing a good job but also because of their diversity. Representing five different denominations, they range from small to large in size. Each is approaching the task of newsletter production from its own unique set of circumstances.

This detailed study should reinforce all the principles you have learned in the other parts of this book and give you some additional ideas for improving your own newsletter.

Case Study #1

First Protestant Vision

Published by: First Protestant Church (United Church of Christ), New Braunfels, Texas
Frequency: Monthly
Format and size: 11½x14″ tabloid, newspaper page format; 8 pages per issue
Printing process: Offset, by an outside printer

This unusual publication is one of the snappiest church papers you'll find anywhere. Its unique newspaper format gives it a timely, streamlined look (see reproduction of front page on p. 100). Wherever it circulates, it attracts attention and makes friends for the church.

For years First Protestant Church had published a two-page, 8½x11″ weekly newsletter, produced first by mimeograph and then by photocopying. But it decided to move to the tabloid monthly format after doing a careful study of church needs and comparing costs. It discovered that the

total production costs for the monthly tabloid were considerably less than those for the weekly two-page mailout. Most of this savings is a result of the lower postage bill for a monthly publication.

What do church members think of the change? Some miss the listing of people in the hospital that was always published weekly before. But besides that, response to the monthly format has been very positive.

The editor of *First Protestant Vision* gets typesetting done for the paper at a local print shop. Then she prepares a complete camera-ready paste-up of the pages. The tabloid printer reduces or enlarges the photos to fit the spaces on the pages, makes the printing plates, and prints about 2,000 copies of each issue. The church mails about 1,400 copies per month to members and uses the additional 600 for membership recruitment and promotion throughout the community. These extra copies cost only a few cents each, and they are excellent as publicity handouts.

This newsletter publishes many fine articles and features (see reproduction, p. 101). In addition to focusing on local church concerns, it also challenges members to get involved in broader community needs and critical social problems. Photographs of top quality are also a real plus of the paper.

Besides articles and photographs, *First Protestant Vision* also publishes several small commercial ads in each issue (see reproduction, p. 101). Tastefully designed and displayed, these ads seem right at home on the tabloid newspaper page. And they bring in a little income each month to help defray the expenses of production.

Case Study #2

The Advocate

Published by: First Church of the Brethren, San Diego, California
Frequency: Monthly
Format and size: 5½x8½″ page size; 12 pages per issue
Printing process: Mimeograph

While it's a mimeographed publication issued by a small church, *The Advocate* is anything but a typical low-budget production. This church squeezes every ounce of potential out of the stencil process to publish a first-class newsletter.

The first thing you notice about its front page (see illustration, p. 102) is the sharp, well-designed masthead at the top. The church had this designed by a professional artist. Then a local printer reproduced the logo on a large supply of mimeo paper stock. The mimeograph operator adds the finishing touch by typing the stencil and using this preprinted paper when running the front page for each issue. It's an excellent technique for putting some sparkle into that all-important first page.

The inside pages of *The Advocate* show this same creative planning and attention to detail that make such a big difference in a mimeographed publication. Notice how the headlines are inset into the copy along the left margin and underlined for contrast. The two illustrations are also worked into the copy like this with just the right amount of white space on all sides. And notice how these art spots are placed at the top and bottom to help break up this gray page. All these techniques together produce a page with excellent eye appeal.

First Church of the Brethren subscribes to the stencil art service provided by its own denomination as well as an additional line of mimeo illustrations from an independent publisher. Occasionally it also sends several pieces of copyright-free art to a mimeograph dealer for conversion to stencil art on an electronic scanner. These three sources keep the newsletter well supplied with good stencil illustrations, which add immeasurably to its visual impact.

The church has also invested in a number of stencil preparation aids to help give its newsletter a more professional look. Notice the large headline over the pastor's column, "The First Word," on the front page of *The Advocate*. This was composed with a stencil letterguide and a stylus. (See chapter 5 for additional information on stencil preparation aids.)

Case Study #3

Newsletter of Southport United Methodist Church, Indianapolis, Indiana

Frequency: Monthly
Format and size: 8½x11″ page size; 10 to 12 pages per issue
Printing process: Photocopying

The newsletter of this suburban church has it all together in a prize-winning package—good editorial content, sparkling illustrations, and attractive page layout and design. What's more, it has an efficient, in-office printing system that turns out flawless copies with no messy inks or chemicals. This church paper is one of many that has made the switch in recent years to copying machine.

The newsletter editor likes the flexibility which the photocopying process brings to page layout and design. First, she types all the body copy and small headlines for the news-

letter in rough form. Then she locates the places on her rough copy where illustrations are needed, roughing in other visual elements such as transfer-type headlines, rules, and boxes. After the entire issue has been roughed out like this, page by page, she types the copy again, this time in finished form. As a final operation, she glues or rubs down all the visual elements in their appropriate places on the typewritten sheets. These paste-up masters then go to the copying machine for clean, convenient duplication.

Take a close look at some of the features from this newsletter (see reproduction, p. 103). They should give you an idea of the flexibility which photocopying can bring to graphic design. All the borders and lines on the page were produced with convenient rub-down borders. The large-type headlines were composed by the newsletter editor from transfer type or an easy-to-use Kroy lettering machine. (See chapter 5 for additional information on transfer type and other paste-up techniques.)

This newsletter is also an interesting case study because the editors are convinced that *more* is not necessarily *best*. Their goal is to reduce the number of pages in the newsletter from ten or twelve per issue to six or eight—perhaps to even four eventually. The staff members of the church believe a streamlined edition of the paper would receive better readership. This would also cut down on postage and paper costs, which are going up much faster these days than the budgets of most churches.

As a part of this "streamlining strategy," the church is encouraging members to use other avenues of promotion, including wall posters, brochures and flyers, and notices on church bulletin boards. Many items that would normally be published in the newsletter are also being shifted to the news and promotion sheet that's inserted in the weekly worship bulletin. They believe the newsletter should be used for promotion of only the most important events and concerns in the life of the church.

Case Study #4

The Broadstreeter

Published by: Broad Street Presbyterian Church, Columbus, Ohio
Frequency: Weekly
Format and size: 5½x8½″ page size; 4 pages per issue
Printing process: Printed on offset press by an outside printer

This sharp, professional church newsletter is printed two pages per side on 8½x11″ paper stock, then folded in the middle to produce a four-page publication. It has several excellent features worthy of emulation by other churches.

Notice the neat, streamlined look of the front page (see illustration, p. 104). The two pieces of artwork on this page are positioned at just the right spots in relationship to the copy and the masthead to give the entire page a pleasing, balanced appearance.

On the negative side, the newsletter masthead could use a more creative approach. The name of the newsletter, *The Broadstreeter*, rather than the name of the church should receive the heavy, bold-type emphasis. But notice that the masthead does take up less than a third of the front page—a proportion that's just about right for this important graphic element.

The inside pages of *The Broadstreeter* (see illustration, p. 104) are also tastefully and harmoniously designed through good placement of headlines, copy, and artwork. Notice the lines of typewriter type are justified (lined up evenly along the right margin)—a feature that presents a neat, uniform appearance. The copy looks like it might have been composed by a professional typesetter, but it was actually typed by the church secretary on an electronic memory typewriter with a proportional spacing feature.

In addition to proportional spacing, this versatile typewriter can also produce boldface type, as illustrated in the two articles from *The Broadstreeter* reproduced on page 104. This is an excellent way to draw special attention to names, speeches, discussion topics, or significant events within the body of an article.

An electronic typewriter with these capabilities is an investment you might consider for your own church. These modern office machines aren't all that expensive, and they can bring a more professional look to the pages of your church publication.

Notice the headlines on the inside page from *The Broadstreeter* (see illustration, p. 104) are typed in all capital letters and underlined for an extra bold look to make them stand out from the rest of the copy. Another impressive feature of these headlines is that they summarize what the articles are about, unlike many newsletters that use *label* headlines without offering specific information. Notice the strong, descriptive verbs in the headlines on this page:

Congregation *Invited*
To Participate

Church-Owned Land
To Be Sold

Seniors *Join* Together
For Christmas Fellowship

Singles *Make* Holiday Plans

Conversations Over Coffee
To Meet on Mondays

Another plus of this fine newsletter is its creative use of small borders and boxes. Notice the two decorative frames around the articles about the church's annual Christmas pageant (see illustrations, p. 104). This is a good attention-getting technique that also adds variety and interest to a page.

One final note about *The Broadstreeter*'s paper stock and ink color. Each issue of the newsletter is printed in a deep dark purple ink on ivory-colored paper. The combination creates a tasteful, distinctive mood that reflects a favorable image for the church. Since this unique combination of ink and paper is used consistently issue after issue, church members recognize the newsletter instantly when it arrives in the mail. This is a real plus in a day when so much reading matter clamors for attention. *The Broadstreeter* is one church newsletter that will definitely not be thrown out with the unopened junk mail.

Case Study #5

Good News!

Published by: Grace Chapel, Tucson, Arizona
Frequency: Weekly
Format and size: 5½x8½" page size; 4 to 8 pages per issue
Printing process: Copy machine

This well-designed weekly newsletter of about 1,500 circulation per issue is a good example of how computer technology can be successfully applied to the publishing process in a church office. Through the marvels of desk-top publishing (see p. 104), the editor of *Good News!* keyboards the manuscript for each issue; designs the pages on a computer screen by typesetting headlines, boxes, and rules; and then prints out the pages in camera-ready form on a laser printer. These typeset pages serve as the master, which is then printed on a copying machine at the rate of about 60 per minute.

The computer hardware which handles this weekly job is a Macintosh computer with an accompanying Apple LaserWriter printer. But the heart of the entire system is the Macintosh version of PageMaker, one of the most popular desk-top publishing software packages on the market today (see p. 108 for address of this software manufacturer).

PageMaker's versatility is demonstrated by the reproduction of a front page and an inside page from *Good News!* (see illustrations on p. 104). All type for these pages, including the small type as well as the headlines, were output easily by PageMaker. A special graphics feature in the software also enables PageMaker to draw the boxes and rules that appear on these two pages. Even the special shaded areas to the left and bottom of the box around the front page were generated by this software.

But the illustration and photographs that appear on these two pages were not output by PageMaker. The newsletter editor placed the type around these illustrations by computer and left "windows" or empty spaces where the illustrations appear. After PageMaker output the pages, the illustrations were placed in these blank spaces by hand. Scanning illustrations and photos electronically into a computer-generated page requires expensive equipment and specialized skills. But breakthroughs in this phase of electronic publishing will probably change this situation dramatically in future years.

For an eye-opening look at page designs of a more complicated nature that can be handled by desk-top publishing, examine the calendar of activities from an issue of *Good News!* (see illustration on p. 104). This page is formatted and printed out every month by using PageMaker and a special graphics software package from Apple Computer known as MacDraw. Many different special graphics packages like these are available from software manufacturers. These graphics add-ons increase the capability of a general desk-top publishing program.

Graphics packages now available include such items as layout forms, fonts of type, award and certificate forms, and clip art logos and symbols. For the most up-to-date list of what's available, check a current software directory or the latest issues of specialized computer magazines at newsstands and bookstores.

Five first-class newsletters—but what a contrast in philosophy, approach, and production processes! It shows that creativity can't be bottled up and then poured out in neat little doses. Each of these congregations used its ingenuity to design a system to meet its needs. Only you can come up with the mix that is just right for your church. Perhaps this book has given you enough information to move you a few steps in that direction.

First Protestant
Vision

"where there is no vision the people perish" Proverbs 29:18

Vol. 1 No. 3
June, 1982

C. Richard Morris To Be Commissioned

Photo by John Senter
New Braunfels Herald

C. Richard Morris, Minister of Music and Fine Arts at First Protestant Church, will become a Commissioned Worker for the United Church of Christ.

UCC Celebrates Silver Anniversary

The birth of the United Church of Christ on June 25, 1957 was recognized by Christian bodies from around the world as having significance in the growing movement of Christian unity shared by all who confess Christ as Lord.

Several characteristics of the parent denominations plus the sensivity to the influence of societal conditions were important in the impast ot the merger.

The Evangelical and Reformed Church and Congregational Christian Churches encompassed very different strands of theology and church policy. The teachings of Calven, Luther, Welsey, Zwingli and left-wing theological perspectives are all identifliable in the histories of these bodies and in the present day congregations. Congregational and presbyterial styles of church organization were modified and blended to develop a continued on page 7

C. Richard Morris, Minister of Music and Fine Arts, will become a Commissioned Worker inthe United Church of Christ at the 10:30 Worship Service Sunday, June 6.

A Commissioned Worker of the United Church of Christ is one of its unordained members who has been called by God and commissioned by the member's association to perform specific church-related service.

Commissioning serves to remind the Commissioned Workers and the Association that the work of the church requires many ministries within the church and in the church's relationship to the world. For the Commissioned Worker, this can serve as a source of strength and as a mode of interpreting the work and its meaning.

First Protestant To Host Workshop

A Music and Arts Workshop is scheduled to take place at First Protestant Church June 17 through the 20.

Workshops, choral reading sessions, and many special events will mark these days as people attend from all over Texas and Louisiana to gather resources and exchange ideas. Claire Smith and Dick Morris head up the South Central Conference Steering Committee who have planned this event. Resource people will include Elizabeth and Roberta Elliott in Drama, Dr. Arlis Hiebert in Choral Reading and Vocal Techniques. Trudie Gregory in the Visual Arts and Dick Morris in Organ. This event is open to people from the South continued on page 4

June Grubb Accepts Conference Position

June Grubb, Minister of Christian Education at First Protestant Church for the past five years will go to Denver, Colorado to accept the position of Associate Conference Minister for Parish Resources for the Rocky Mountain Conferenc.

New Orleans Hosts SCC

The theme banner which hung in the Chancel of the Chapel where all of the business meetings took place, was the work of Mrs. Susan Garman and Mrs. Betsie Tremant.

by Friedrich Rest

At the South Central Conference Annual Meeting held in New Orleans May 21-23, two messages on "Created to be Whole: Whole Persons, Whole Families, Whole World" were given by Dr. Malcom Warford, new President of Eden Theological Seminary, Webster Groves, Missouri. The Rev. Joseph Evans, now serving his 15th year as Secretary of the denomination, gave an opening address on the first evening of the conference, with the sermon on Sunday morning by the Rev. Frederick T. Schumacher, pastor of St. Matthew Church, New Orleans on the "Whole World" aspect. The quality of these inspirational addresses and sermons was up to high expectations! Hymn singing was inspiring too!

Two from our church had major leadership responsibilities; Mrs. laverne (Leon) Eberhard was the moderator of the conference and C. continued on page 4

June Grubb has accepted the invitation of the Rocky Mountain Conference of the United Church of Christ to join the professional staff as Associate Conference Minister for Parish Resources. The Rocky Mountain Conference consists of ninety-nine congregations with a total of 23,923 members in Colorado, Wyoming and Utah. Ms. Grubb's primary responsibilities in her new positon will include Christian education, lay ministries, women's youth and other special ministries, family life, camping, leadership development and Christian nurture. In addition to those she will assist the conference minister in the delivery of pastoral care and placement service. She will also be engaged in speaking, preaching and writing to help the church's ministry.

June's resignation from the staff of First Protestant Church will become effective July 31, 1982. Her departure date will mark exactly five years as Minister of Christian Education here. During these five years the Christian Education program at First Protestant Church has grown. Workshops and leadership training have been priorities of June's leadership. A day care program was instituted under her leadership. She has given direction to many dramatic productions, i.e., chancel drama, Christmas and Easter pageants, and major productions involving the entire Church School in cooperation with the music ministry in the productions of "Joseph..." and "Noah..."

June's departure will leave a large gap in the life of First Protestant Church. Many continued on page 3

Front Page of *First Protestant Vision*

Children's Corner

DOWN

1. The person who usually preaches in church is called a _____ (plural).
2. These persons sing special music in the worship service.
3. All persons who believe in Jesus are called _____
4. These persons are elected to be the leaders of the church
7. Eighteen persons who help others who are sick or needy.
9. The person who called the first disciples to follow him.

ACROSS

5. The first followers of Jesus were called _____
6. The special book that persons study in the church.
8. All persons who belong to the church.
10. The one who plays the organ and leads the choir.
11. All children, youth and adult classes are led by __.
12. Persons who go to many places in the world to preach, teach, heal, and help others.

(Crossword grid: PERSONS IN THE CHURCH)

Youth To Be Confirmed On Penecost Sunday

On May 30, thirty-seven young people, who are in eighth and ninth grade, will be confirmed in the membership of First Protestant Church.

These young people have spent this school year, beginning in August, 1981, in special studies, using the new UCC Confirmation Resource, "Confirming Our Faith".

We are looking at the possibility of dividing the class into two sections, so that part of the class would be confirmed at 8:00 a.m. and the other half at 10:30 a.m. on May 30. This will be subject to the wishes of the youth and their parents.

The Church Life Committee will host a reception on the Bormann Room at 9:15 a.m. for the confirmands and their parents and sponsors.

This year's class includes Eighth graders, Jana Chafin, Jim Dean, Sandra Haecker, Barbara Hummel, Jeff Kohlenberg, Christopher Kroesche, Faye Meckel, Leah Morton, Cara Nowotny, Tracy Odell, Candy Osteen, Sonya Peek, Nathan Pfeil, Ray Pfeuffer, Jacqueline Schaefer, Karen Ward, Lisa Wetz and Charles Wimberley. Ninth graders are Julie Bartling, Bruce Blang, Sharon Borgfeld, Melissa Combs, James Damerau, Paul Dean, Michele Doepenschmidt, Kristina Flowers, Elgen Froboese, Troy Heitkamp, Kenan Ikels, Roger Koening, Lee Jay Luehlfing, David Putz, Shannon Reinhard, Patricia Scheffel, Brenda Thiele, Glynda Thiele, and Mark Wimberley.

Neighbors In Need Sunday Scheduled For October 3

Neighbors In Need

The neighobors in Need offering is an annual all-church offering to support programs in the United States among disadvantaged people, through the homeland instrumentalities and agencies of the United Church of Christ.

To act justly toward one's neighbor, to assist the poor and needy, is not simply a matter of mere humanity. Both the Old Testament and the New Testament make abundantly clear that sharing one's possessions with a neighbor in need is to obey God in faith. To refuse to share is to act idolatrously; it is a breaking of the covenantal relationship we have with God.

Thus, our annual Neighbors in Need all-church offering is part of our keeping of the covenant with

God by sharing with persons in special need. Children in want, the handicapped without rights, immigrants seeking opportunity, and minorities in need of justice are among those with whom we have shared and are still sharing.

The 1982 Neighbors in Need offering will make possible further sharing as follows:

*$132,500 to the Commission for Racial Justice for "Ministry to Battered Wives and their families."
*$150,00 to the United Church Board for Homeland Ministries for "Empowerment for Persons in Depressed Regions."
*$40,000 to the Office of Communication for "TV Spots Linking Hunger to World Peace."
*$150,000 to the United Church Board for Homeland Ministries for "Volunteers in Service to Human Need."
*$173,000 to the Office for Church in Society for "Advocacy for Families Victimized by Federal Budget Cuts."
*$150,000 to the United Church Board for Homland

Scenes Around First Protestant Church

The Castro Home purchased by the First Protestant Church as a youth center in 1958, now houses Sunday morning Church School classes as well as the Kindergarten/Day Care Center.

Third Graders Receive Bibles

Twelve Church School students were given Bibles on Sunday, August 29 at the 10:30 worship service. Each year the students who are entering third grade are honored in this way. Those receiving their Bibles were Brandon Dietert, Jessica Harmes, Jonathan Jarrett, Wade Lindemann, Teri Logan, Karla Ormond, Sarah Parsley, Michelle Pierce, Lisa Rauch, Lisa Osteen, Michael Plumeyer and Christy Westbrook.

Party Honors Kennedys

Rev. and Mrs. J. Linwood Kennedy prepare to leave after after worship services on Sunday, June 20 for a vacation trip to a cabin in the mountains of North Carolina. The trip and a reception were a surprise from a group of friends and family for their twenty-fifth wedding anniversary.

Rev. and Mrs. J. Linwood Kennedy were honored Sunday, June 13, with a surprise twenty-fifth wedding anniversary party at the Faust Hotel by a group of close friends and family.

Master of Ceremonies for the afternoon, Dick Morris, touched on the highlights of the honored couple's life together and introduced their five children, Mary Lynn, John, Mark, Laura and Amy. A special feature of the afternoon was a duet played by Mary Lynn Kennedy on the flute and Marion Fischer on Classical guitar.

The highlight of the afternoon was the opening of their anniversary gift, a six day trip to the mountains of North Carolina, paid for by contributions from many of their friends.

Federal Budget Cuts Aid For Needy

A federal budget for 1983 passed June 10 by the House of Representatives has been characterized by the leaders of 25 religious bodies as "unconscionable and deceptive destruction of 50 years of social progress". The Rev. Paul Kittlaus, a United Church of Christ minister who chairs the Interreligious Emergency continued on page 7

Semi-Annual Meeting Set For September

The Fall Semi-Annual Congregational Meeting has been scheduled for Sunday, September 26 following the 10:30 worship service. At this meeting a report on the success of the Pony Express Stewardship Program will be given. A financial update on the 1982 budget will also be presented. Other progress reports on areas of interest to the congregation will be a part of the agenda.

Just a Few of *Vision's* Fine Articles and Features

Small Ads Help Defray the Cost of Publication

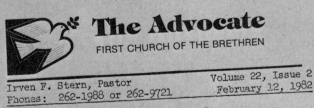

The Advocate
FIRST CHURCH OF THE BRETHREN

Irven F. Stern, Pastor	Volume 22, Issue 2
Phones: 262-1988 or 262-9721	February 12, 1982

THE FIRST WORD

In January and February this year Epiphany has been a major theme in worship experiences. It lifts up Scriptural themes that speak of Jesus being revealed to the Gentiles, to the Jews, to nature and to ourselves. Acknowledging Jesus as Messiah and becoming aware of his Lordship over nature takes a great deal of faith.

On Sunday, February 14, we will see that Jesus came to preach the Good News but he allowed his preaching mission to be interrupted by persons with special physical needs. In Mark's gospel we read of a leper who came to Jesus to be made clean (1:40-45). Jesus was not too busy. On February 21 the story of Jesus' Transfiguration (Mark 9:2-9) will dominate our worship theme. The last Sunday in February will be the first Sunday in Lent. We will serve Holy Communion in the worship service. The focus will be on God's love [for] us as shown in Jesus Christ.

Growing out of a suggestion by David Warren we are developing a special Lenten study/worship series on the theme "JESUS IS LORD". In the primitive church this was the confession of every believer, made at the time of baptism. The Christian Education committee has approved making this a topic for study by adults of our congregation during the Church School hour for each Sunday in March. [We] urge each adult in our fellowship to join in for [an] in-depth study of what our baptismal confession, "Jesus Is Lord", means. The worship services [will] build on each study theme.

Front Page of *The Advocate*

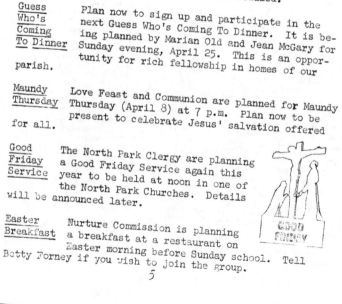

Appreciation To Dollie Clark for purchase of shades covering the large windows in the sanctuary, and to Ben Clark for installing them. These will cut down the fading of the carpet and chairs by about 90% and cut the glare for those facing the windows.

Wanted Church Board is looking for someone, or a couple in our congregation to represent us on the Camp LaVerne Board. If you are interested in serving in this way speak to Betty Forney soon. Emma Rachow has served in this capacity for a couple of years. Our deep appreciation to her.

Join Church Membership Class Pastor Stern is interested in beginning a class for persons interested in church membership. If you or someone you know is interested in being in such a class to learn about the meaning of membership in this church please tell him so that a class can be scheduled.

Guess Who's Coming To Dinner Plan now to sign up and participate in the next Guess Who's Coming To Dinner. It is being planned by Marian Old and Jean McGary for Sunday evening, April 25. This is an opportunity for rich fellowship in homes of our parish.

Maundy Thursday Love Feast and Communion are planned for Maundy Thursday (April 8) at 7 p.m. Plan now to be present to celebrate Jesus' salvation offered for all.

Good Friday Service The North Park Clergy are planning a Good Friday Service again this year to be held at noon in one of the North Park Churches. Details will be announced later.

Easter Breakfast Nurture Commission is planning a breakfast at a restaurant on Easter morning before Sunday school. Tell Betty Forney if you wish to join the group.

5

Inside Page of *The Advocate*

NEWS OF OUR MEMBERS AND FRIENDS

EVELYN EMERSON, wife of our Music Director, is now accepting piano students. Contact Evelyn at 887-1451 for information.

NEEDED--Babysitter for 3-month old daughter of Jim and Susan Wycoff beginning in mid-November for 30 hours per week, Mon. thru Friday. Contact Susan at 881-1742.

THE CEILING IS NO LONGER FALLING AT SUMC! Thanks to Malcolm McNeil and Ken Poole for their hard work in repairing the unsightly hole in the office restroom.

Sunday, Oct. 31 has been designated as ALL SAINTS DAY at SUMC. Those in our church family who have died within the last year will be remembered. The altar bouquet will include a white carnation in memory of each person. Those who are to be remembered are: Hannah Irish, Sarah Elaine Biszantz, Steven Outcalt, Frank McClellan, Carolyn Beck, Roy Beals, Janet Thompson and Evelyn Adams.

PASTOR SCHWEIN spoke on "Career Day" at Perry Meridian High School to students who were interested in entering the ministry.

When the Every Member Commitment Program planning committee met on Sept. 26 a tremendous amount of enthusiasm was aroused by The Circuit Rider plan. As details unfolded, committee members agreed that the simplicity of the plan, its strong emphasis on biblical stewardship, and its being just plain fun will help make this year's funding campaign the most successful ever.

Alva Funk, General Overseer of The Circuit Rider plan, announced that November 14 has been set as Circuit Rider Sunday.

November 14 set as Circuit Rider Sunday.

This year's goal is 100 percent member participation and pledges of $274,514 to support our church's ministry for the coming year.

Circuits have been drawn up by geographical area, and Circuit Leaders will begin calling members in each area soon to explain the plan. Alva emphasized that while each household will be invited to send out a Circuit Rider, other opportunities for participation are available to those who can't ride a circuit.

DINNER AND MEETING FOR WORK AREAS & ADMINISTRATIVE BOARD

TUESDAY, OCTOBER 19

6:00 p.m. Dinner
6:30 p.m. Work Area meetings
8:00 p.m. Administrative Board

Work Areas and Committees meeting are:
Education
Mission
Evangelism
Race & Religion
Finance
Church & Society
Worship
Christian Unity
(Chairpersons will be contacting their committees.)

The cost of the dinner will be $2.50/person and reservations must be phoned into the church office by Wednesday, October 13.

"THE HILLS ARE ALIVE WITH THE SOUND OF MUSIC"

If this is one of your favorites, join the 50 PLUS CLUB on Wednesday, October 6. The group will leave on the church bus at 10:30 a.m. for the Beef 'n Boards Dinner Theatre. The cost of the tickets will be $11 which includes lunch. Wendell Church will be driving the bus, and there is plenty of room. Bring a friend along.

Southport United Methodist Church—
Strong Graphic Elements for a Winning Design

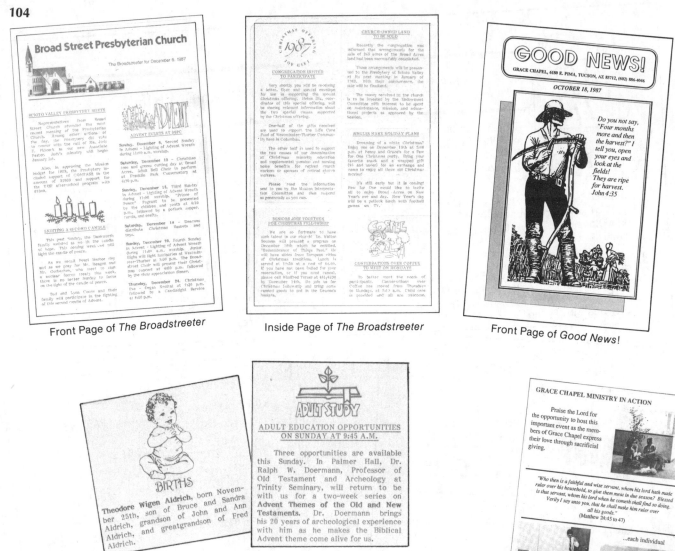

Front Page of *The Broadstreeter*

Inside Page of *The Broadstreeter*

Front Page of *Good News!*

Highlighting Important Facts with Boldface Type

Inside Page of *Good News!*

Monthly Calendar of Church Activities Produced by Computer and Laser Printer

The Broadstreeter's Creative Use of Small Boarders and Boxes

11
Specialized Resources
to Simplify Newsletter Production

Publishing a good newsletter issue after issue calls for many specialized materials—clip art, stencils, layout sheets, transfer type, etc. You will find these resources at Christian book stores, art supply firms, and duplicating equipment dealers in many cities. Look under these subject headings in the yellow pages of your telephone directory to find local suppliers. Then call or visit to see what specialized resources they offer.

In addition to local outlets, contact the following suppliers that do business by mail. Ask for copies of their catalogs, brochures, or fliers with full descriptions of their products or services. Use these specialized materials to bring a fresh, bright look to your newsletter.

Clip Art

All Church Technical Services, 1640 Rockwood Trail, Fayetteville, Arkansas 72701. Fresh artwork at reasonable prices on scores of subjects, including Bible study, fellowship, worship, stewardship, music, missions, discipleship, family, and recreation.

The Church Art Works, 875 High St., N.E., Salem, Oregon 97301. A quarterly clip art subscription service offering fresh, contemporary artwork in the expensive price range.

College Press Publishing, P.O. Box 1132, Joplin, Missouri 64802. A clip art subscription service, mailed either monthly or quarterly. Good art work, but relatively expensive.

Communication Resources, P.O. Box 2625, North Canton, Ohio 44720. Clip art on dozens of themes and subjects, with special emphasis on youth, cartoons, and large format art spots for church bulletin covers. Other popular subjects treated are worship, family, music, children, camping, and communion.

Creative Christian Clip Art, 5701 Slide Rd., #C-123, Lubbock, Texas 79414. A quarterly clip art subscription service, offering art on such topics as music, Sunday School, holidays, and revival.

Creative Communications, P.O. Box 55588, Jackson, Mississippi 39216. A good source for youth and church recreation clip art.

Creative Media Services, P.O. Box 5955, Berkeley, California 94705. All clip art offered by this service is drawn in a humorous, cartoon style. Particularly appealing to churches are the clip art books on people, holidays, special events, animals, and sports.

Crown National Bureau, 424 N. 3rd St., Burlington, Iowa 52601. Quality clip art in individually priced books on such subjects as youth, senior adults, holidays, and stewardship.

Gene Johnson Productions, P.O. Box 3520, Estes Park, Colorado 80517. Specialty clip art, with a music orientation, for use in the music ministry of a church.

Knight Media, 60 Benzing Rd., Antioch, Tennessee 37013. More than 50 clip art books from several different publishers, carefully selected to fill the specialized needs of churches. Also available are several low-priced books of borders and panels, clip art cartoons, sentence sermons, and illustrated fillers and essays to spark up your church publications.

Logos Art Productions, 346 Chester St., St. Paul, Minnesota 55107. This firm offers small-format illustrations on holidays, Bible events, and special days on the church calendar. Also offered are the official symbols or logos of several major denominations in clip art format.

Norman H. Ludlow, Publisher, 516 Arnett Blvd., Rochester, New York 14619. An excellent resource for clip art books in the moderate price range on such subjects as sports and recreation, youth, people, holidays, family, camping, and outdoors.

Mission Media, P.O. Box 1149, Orange Park, Florida 32067. Several volumes of church clip art on many different subjects, including Easter, evangelism, food, prayer, worship, and special days.

Neibauer Press, 20 Industrial Dr., Warminster, Pennsylvania 18974. Several different volumes of general church art in the low price range.

New Generation Art Pak, 9201 N.E. Fremont, Portland Oregon 97220. A clip art service offering fresh, contemporary material on a variety of subjects at a reasonable price.

Brad Price Design Studio, 2825 Bledsoe St., Fort Worth, Texas 76107. A clip art subscription service that offers new art spots to subscribers periodically throughout the year. All subscription services are expensive, and you receive a lot of art you never use. This firm is worth investigating, however, if you are willing to pay a premium price for a steady supply of fresh materials.

The Printers Shopper, P.O. Drawer 1056, Chula Vista, California 92012. A good source of ready-to-use borders, cartoons, and clip art on such subjects as sports, holidays, and travel. Ask for their latest general catalog of printing supplies.

Nido R. Qubein & Associates, P.O. Box 5367, High Point, North Carolina 27262. This company offers seasonal and general clip art as well as a wide range of cartoons for church bulletins and newsletters.

Thou Art, P.O. Box 671374, Dallas, Texas 75367. This service offers a one-volume collection of general clip art on scores of subjects.

The Vary Idea, P.O. Box 640, Grapevine, Texas 76051. Each year this company issues a new volume of clip art on many subjects—an ideal clip-and-use resource at a reasonable price. Also available is a one-volume collection of church music clip art.

Visuals in Ministry, 3726 Cavalier, Garland, Texas 75042. A new compilation of church clip art is issued each year. Subjects covered by the art spots include outreach, senior adults, holidays, Bible study, music, and missions.

Whelan's Church Art, P.O. Box 662, Canyon, Texas 79015. A good subscription service which offers quality clip art in the moderate price range.

Graphic Arts and Printing Supplies

Alignmate, 7375 E. Stetson Dr., Ste. 103, Scottsdale, Arizona 85251. This firm sells a low-cost, see-through plastic grid that allows you to check pasteups for straightness before printing. A handy time- and money-saving tool for every church office.

Communication Resources, P.O. Box 2625, North Canton, Ohio 44720. A full line of newsletter production supplies, including layout pasteup forms, transfer type, clip art, and copyright-free Bible crossword puzzles for publication in your church newsletter.

Dot Pasteup Supply Co., P.O. Box 369, Omaha, Nebraska 68101. This company sells everything you need to produce professional-quality pasteups for all your church publications. Supplies include layout grids, specialty papers, light tables, templates, graphic arts rulers and knives, ink, pens, transfer type, and cutting boards.

In House Graphics, 342 E. 3rd St., Loveland, Colorado 80537. This company specializes in bringing you the latest information and easy-to-use software in the growing field of desktop publishing—the application of the personal computer to such functions as typesetting and page design. Ask for their latest catalog of desk-top publishing supplies.

The Printers Shopper, P.O. Drawer 1056, Chula Vista, California 92012. An excellent buy-by-mail source for hard-to-find printing supplies, including hand-operated binding machines, paper folders, tabletop light tables, precision measuring rules, pens and markers, specialty stapling machines, transfer type, glues and adhesives, pasteup supplies, and clip art borders and general illustrations.

Newsletters and Magazines

Christian Computer News, published by the Christian Computer Users Association, P.O. Box 7344, Grand Rapids, Michigan 49510. If your church office is computerized, or even if you are thinking of moving in this direction, consider joining this national organization. Its official newsletter will keep you informed of the latest developments in computer software for church use and the trends in application·of the computer to typical church office tasks.

Church Administration, 127 Ninth Ave., N., Nashville, Tennessee 37234. A monthly publication for pastors, church secretaries, and other staff members of local churches. It publishes helpful articles on public relations, communications, and newsletter production techniques.

The Churchmouse, 1909 Texas, Norman, Oklahoma 73071. The articles in this publication consist of illustrated parables with a moral lesson spoken in the unique style of "the churchmouse." Issued monthly in camera-ready format. Local church subscribers may publish the ready-to-use articles from *The Churchmouse* in their own newsletters and bulletins.

Church Secretary's Communique, P.O. Box 2301, Matthews, North Carolina 28106. A monthly magazine devoted exclusively to the work of the church secretary, with helpful articles on office management, working with people, and producing the church newsletter and other publications.

The DeskTop, 342 E. 3rd St., Loveland, Colorado 80537. A monthly newsletter that brings you "inside information" on the latest developments in desktop publishing.

Memo to Mailers, P.O. Box 999, Springfield, Virginia 22150. A monthly publication of the Postal Service, provided free to high-volume users of the U.S. Mail. It provides tips on how to use the bulk mailing system more effectively. Write on your church letterhead and ask to be placed on the mailing list.

The Newsletter Newsletter, P.O. Box 2625, North Canton, Ohio 44720. A monthly publication for local churches that features tips and techniques to help you produce a first-class church newsletter. In addition to how-to-do-it articles, each issue also contains printed fillers and artwork that can be clipped and published in local church publications.

Publish! PCW Communications, Inc., 501 2nd St., San Francisco, California 94107. A monthly magazine, available on newsstands as well as by subscription, devoted exclusively to the specialized subject of desktop publishing. An excellent resource on the very latest in this growing industry, including software, hardware, graphics, and design innovations, etc.

The Vary Idea, P.O. Box 640, Grapevine, Texas 76051. A monthly publication featuring the best ideas for promoting church attendance, Bible study, stewardship, church growth, training, etc. These ideas are gleaned from churches of all denominations throughout the United States on a systematic basis. Each issue of this informative publication also publishes two pages of clip art for church newsletter editors.

Church Management Software Systems

Chapter 9 of this book (see pages 92-95) discusses the application of the personal computer to church newsletter production. Typesetting and page layout and design by computer are now possible in the church office. To perform these tasks, you will need a laser printer and a special desktop publishing software package.

The following firms specialize in providing total computer software systems to churches for many different functions—maintaining membership records, keeping up with contributions, doing word processing, producing mailing labels for mass mailings, etc. Many of these companies are also adding desktop publishing programs to their software packages. Write these firms for information about the specific functions which their software packages will perform.

Adam Church Management System, AdamSoft, Inc., 115 N. Neil St., Champaign, Illinois 61820.

Angel Systems, Inc., 1967 Hazen St., Jackson Heights, New York 11370.

Applied Computer Systems, Inc., 2175 Germantown Rd., Ste. 304, Germantown, Tennessee 38138.

The Ark, CISCO Computer Systems, 1117 Loop 304, E., Crockett, Texas 75835.

Automated Church System, Computer Dimensions, 1803 Cherokee Rd., Ste. 201, Florence, South Carolina 29501.

Automated Records Management System (ARMS), Mission Techniques, Inc., P.O. Box 15864, Chattanooga, Tennessee 37415.

Brother John Software Systems, CompuData, Inc., 10501 Drummond Rd., Philadelphia, Pennsylvania 19154.

Church Administrative Program Service (CAPS), WEB Data Corporation, 2930 Flowers Rd., S., Atlanta, Georgia 30341.

Church Business Manager, CP Software, 1501 Adams Ave., Milpitas, California 95035.

Church Graceware, P.O. Box JA, College Station, Texas 77841.

Church Information Management Program (CHIMP), Church Management Systems, 2919 Grand River Dr., N.E., Grand Rapids, Michigan 49505.

Church Information Management System, Genesis Computer Systems, 7370 Opportunity Rd., Ste. H, San Diego, California 92111.

Church Information System (CIS), Sunday School Board, 127 Ninth Ave., N., Nashville, Tennessee 37234.

Church Management System, MSI Membership Services, P.O. Box 152130, Irving, Texas 75015.

Church Management Systems, Software Library, 3300 County Rd. 10, Ste. 304, Brooklyn Center, Minnesota 55429.

Church Manager, Titus Information Systems, 3027 W. Indian School Rd., Phoenix, Arizona 85017.

Church/Mate, Mid-Valley Computer Services, P.O. Box 2445, Oakhurst, California 93644.

Church Organizational Management System, Specialty Software, P.O. Box 5494, Evansville, Indiana 47715.

Church Records Management System, Three Pro Computer Systems, 701 E. Lincolnway, Valparaiso, Indiana 46383.

Church Resource Information System (CRIS), National Church Supply Co., P.O. Box 269, Chester, Virginia 26034.

CompuChurch, MTS, Inc., P.O. Box 596, Niceville, Florida 32578.

CRISS Church Management Software Solution, Samuelson Associates, 350 S. Schmale Rd., Carol Stream, Illinois 60188.

EZ Systems, P.O. Box 23190, Nashville, Tennessee 37202.

Episcopal Church Information System (ECIS), 1661 N. Northwest Hwy., Park Ridge, Illinois 60068

Genesis Software, Hunter Systems, 8-D Watertown Circle, Birmingham, Alabama 35235.

Heaven Cent Software, Stein Enterprises, 1606 Evers Dr., McLean, Virginia 22101.

Integrated Church Management System (ICMS), Omega C. G. Limited, 1100 31st St., Downers Grove, Illinois 60515.

Interactive Church Information System (ICIS), AGC Corporation, 170 N. Ocoee St., Cleveland, Tennessee 37311.

Little Shepherd System, RMS Technology, 9680 S. Gribble Rd., Canby, Oregon 97013.

Local Church Computer System (LCCS), Computer Helper, 6495 Sawmill Rd., Dublin, Ohio 43017.

Logos, Lowell Brown Enterprises, 6025 Nicolle St., Ventura, California 93003.

Lutheran Congregational Information System (LCIS), Fortress Press, 2900 Queen Lane, Philadelphia, Pennsylvania 19129.

Parish Data System, 3140 N. 51st Ave., Phoenix, Arizona 85031.

Power Church Plus, F1 Software, P.O. Box 3096, Beverly Hills, California 90212.

Presbyterian Church Information System (PCIS), 1661 N. Northwest Hwy., Park Ridge, Illinois 60068.

RJM Software, 104 E. 7th St., Hanford, California 93230.

Renewed Software, 3 Charleston, Irvine, California 92720.

Romar Church Systems, P.O. Box 4211, Elkhart, Indiana 46514.

The Servant, Corinthian Software, 3616 Trimble Rd., Nashville, Tennessee 37215.

108

HOW TO PUBLISH A CHURCH NEWSLETTER

Shelby Church System, 5865 Hyatt Ridgeway Pkwy., Ste. 105, Memphis, Tennessee 38119.

Shepherd, Shepherd Systems, Inc., 1713 Mahan Dr., Tallahassee, Florida 32308.

Toleco, Inc., P.O. Box 6496, Woodland Hills, California 91365.

United Methodist Information System (UMIS/Plus), 1661 N. Northwest Hwy., Park Ridge, Illinois 60068.

Manufacturers of Label-Applying Machines

Chapter 8 of this book (see pages 87-91) mentions label-applying machines that cut down on the time involved in applying computer-generated pressure-sensitive labels to your church newsletter by hand. Write the following manufacturers for information about labeling equipment and the names and locations of local dealers.

Dispensamatic Label Dispensers, 1335 Convention Plaza, St. Louis, Missouri 63103.

Hallie Label Machines, P.O. Box 15338, Chattanooga, Tennessee 37415.

Heyer, Inc., 1850 S. Kostner Ave., Chicago, Illinois 60623.

Master Addresser Company, 7506 W. 27th St., Minneapolis, Minnesota 55426.

Postalia, Inc., 1423 Centre Circle Dr., Downers Grove, Illinois 60515.

Copying Machine Manufacturers

Chapter 7 of this book (see pages 82-86) discusses several points to consider if you are using a copying machine to produce your newsletter or thinking about buying one to perform this task. Write the following manufacturers for information about their copying machines and the names and locations of local dealers.

Adler-Royal Business Machines, P.O. Box 1597, Union, New Jersey 07083.

A. B. Dick, 5700 W. Touhy Ave., Chicago, Illinois 60648.

Eastman Kodak Co., 343 State St., Rochester, New York 14650.

Gestetner Corporation, Gestetner Park, Yonkers, New York 10703.

Harris/3M, 2300 Parklake Dr., N.E., Atlanta, Georgia 30345.

IBM Corporation, Old Orchard Park, Armonk, New York 10504.

Konica-Royal Business Machines, 500 Day Hill Rd., Windsor, Connecticut 06095.

Minolta Corporation, 101 Williams Dr., Ramsey, New Jersey 07446.

Multigraphics, 1800 W. Central Rd., Mt. Prospect, Illinois 60056.

Océ Business Systems, 6500 N. Lincoln Ave., Chicago, Illinois 60645.

Panasonic, Inc., 1 Panasonic Way, Secaucus, New Jersey 07094.

Pitney-Bowes, 1 Elmcroft, Stamford, Connecticut 06926.

Ricoh Corporation, 5 Dederick Pl., West Caldwell, New Jersey 07074.

Sanyo Corporation, 51 Joseph St., Moonachie, New Jersey 07006.

Savin Corporation, 9 W. Broad St., Stamford, Connecticut 06904.

Sharp Electronics, 10 Sharp Plaza, Paramus, New Jersey 07652.

Standard Duplicating Machines, 10 Connector Rd., Andover, Massachusetts 01810.

Toshiba America, Inc., 2441 Michelle Dr., Tustin, California 92680.

Xerox Corporation, Xerox Square, Rochester, New York 14644.

Desktop Publishing Software Packages

Chapter 9 of this book (see pages 92-95) discusses the use of the computer in church newsletter production. The most sophisticated use of the computer involves the typesetting and design of the pages of your newsletter with full-featured desktop publishing software systems. Contact the following suppliers for information about their desktop publishing programs. The names by which these programs or software packages are known precede the names of their manufacturers in this list.

Byline, Ashton-Tate, Inc., 20101 Hamilton Ave., Torrance, California 90502.

City Desk, MicroSearch, Inc., 9896 Southwest Fwy., Houston, Texas 77074.

First Impression, Magahaus Corp., 6215 Ferris Square, San Diego, California 92121.

FrontPage, Studio Software Corp., 17862-C Fitch St., Irvine, California 92714.

Gem Desktop Publisher, Digital Research, Inc., P.O. Box DRI, Monterey, California 93942.

MacPublisher, Boston Software, 1260 Boylston St., Boston, Massachusetts 02215.

The Office Publisher, Laser Friendly, Inc., 930 Benicia Ave., Sunnyvale, California 94086.

PageBuilder, White Sciences, Inc., 2 W. Almeda, Tempe, Arizona 85282.

PageMaker, Aldus Corporation, 411 1st Ave., S., Ste. 200, Seattle, Washington 98104.

PagePerfect, International Microcomputer Software, Inc., 1299 4th St., San Rafael, California 94901.

PageWriter, The 'Puter Group, 1717 N. Beltline Hwy., Madison, Wisconsin 53713.

PS Compose, PS Publishing, Inc., 290 Green St., Ste. 1, San Francisco, California 94133.

Professional Publisher, Software Publishing Corp., 1901 Landings Dr., Mountain View, California 94039.

Quark Xpress, Quark, Inc., 2525 W. Evans, Ste. 220, Denver, Colorado 80219.

Ready, Set, Go! Letraset USA, 40 Eisenhower Dr., Paramus, New Jersey 07653.

Ragtime 2.0, Orange Micro, Inc., 1400 N. Lakeview Ave., Anaheim, California 92807.

Scoop, Target Software, Inc., 14206 S.W. 136th St., Miami, Florida 33186.

Spellbinder Desktop Publisher, Lexisoft, Inc., P.O. Box 1950, Davis, California 95617.

Ventura Publisher, Xerox, Inc., P.O. Box 24, Rochester, New York 14692.

Manufacturers
of Laser Printers

Chapter 9 of this book (see pages 92-95) discusses the use of the computer to produce the church newsletter. A high-resolution laser printer is essential if you want to produce camera-ready copy for the pages of your newsletter in typeset format. Write the following manufacturers for information about their laser printers and the names and locations of local dealers.

Acer Technologies Corporation, 410 Charcot Ave., San Jose, California 95131.

Apple Computer, Inc., 20525 Mariana Ave., Cupertino, California 95014.

AST Research, Inc., 2121 Alton Ave., Irvine, California 92714.

A T & T, 1 Speedwell Ave., Morristown, New Jersey 07960.

BDS, Inc., 800 Maude Ave., Mountain View, California 94043.

Blaser Industries, 6383 Arizona Circle, Los Angeles, California 90045.

Brother International Corporation, 8 Corporate Pl., Piscataway, New Jersey 08855.

C. Itoh Electronics, 19500 S. Hamilton, Torrance, California 90248.

Canon U.S.A., 1 Canon Plaza, Lake Success, New York 11042.

Citizen America, 2401 Colorado Ave., Ste. 190, Santa Monica, California 90404.

Compugraphic Corporation, 200 Ballarduale St., Wilmington, Massachusetts 01887.

DataProducts Corporation, 6200 Canoga Ave., Woodland Hills, California 91365.

Data Recording Systems, 80 Ruland Rd., Melville, New York 11747.

Datasouth Computer Corporation, 4216 Stuart Andrew Blvd., Charlotte, North Carolina 28210.

Data Technology Corporation, 2551 Walsh Ave., Santa Clara, California 95051.

Decision Data Computers, 400 Horsham Rd., Horsham, Pennsylvania 19044.

Digital Equipment Corporation, 129 Parker St., Maynard, Maryland 01754.

Eastman Kodak Co., 343 State St., Rochester, New York 14650.

Epson America, Inc., 2780 Lomita Blvd., Torrance, California 90505.

Facit, Inc., P.O. Box 334, Merrimack, New Hampshire 03054.

Fujitsu America, Inc., 3055 Orchard Dr., San Jose, California 95134.

Genicom Corporation, 1 General Electric Dr., Waynesboro, Virginia 22980.

Hewlett-Packard, 1820 Embarcadero Rd., Palo Alto, California 94303.

IBM Corporation, Old Orchard Park, Armonk, New York 10504.

Imagen Corporation, 2650 San Tomas Expwy, Santa Clara, California 95052.

Kanematus-Gosho, Inc., 333 S. Hope St., Ste. 2800, Los Angeles, California 90071.

Kaypro Computers, 533 Stevens Ave., Solana Beach, California 92075.

Kyocera Unison, Inc., 3165 Adeline St., Berkeley, California 94703.

Mannesman Tally Corporation, 8301 S. 180th St., Kent, Washington 98032.

NEC Corporation, 1414 Massachusetts Ave., Boxboro, Massachusetts 01719.

Okidata, 532 Fellowship Rd., Mt. Laurel, New Jersey 08054.

Olivetti U.S.A., 765 U.S. Hwy. 202, Somerville, New Jersey 08876.

Panasonic Industries, 2 Panasonic Way, Secaucus, New Jersey 07094.

Personal Computer Products, 11590 W. Bernardo Ct., Ste. 100, San Diego, California 92127.

Printronix, Inc., P.O. Box 19559, Irvine, California 92714.

QMS, Inc., 1 Magnum Pass, Mobile, Alabama 36618.

Quadrum Corporation, 1 Quad Way, Norcross, Georgia 30093.

Qume Corporation, 2350 Qume Dr., San Jose, California 95131.

Ricoh Corporation, 5 Dedrick Pl., West Caldwell, New Jersey 07006.

Sharp Electronics, 10 Sharp Plaza, Mahwah, New Jersey 07430.

Siemens Mfg. Co., 410 W. Washington, Freeburg, Illinois 62243.

Star Micronics America, 200 Park Ave., Ste. 3510, New York, New York 10166.

Talaris Systems, 6059 Cornerstone Ct., W., San Diego, California 92121.

Tandy Corporation, 1800 One Tandy Center, Fort Worth, Texas 76102.

Texas Instruments, P.O. Box 809063, Dallas, Texas 75380.

Toshiba America, 9740 Irvine Blvd., Irvine, California 92718.

Varityper, 11 Mt. Pleasant Ave., East Hanover, New Jersey 07936.

Wang Laboratories, 1 Industrial Ave., Lowell, Massachusetts 01851.

Xerox Corporation, Xerox Square, Rochester, New York 14644.

12
Easy-Reference Style Guide for Newsletter Editors

Every church newsletter editor should have a style guide close at hand when writing articles for the paper or typing the final copy. A style guide or checklist is a real time saver. It automatically tells you how to abbreviate, capitalize, and punctuate the written material in your newsletter. Following a uniform style guide also gives your paper a consistency in language usage that comes across as more professional to your readers.

For best results, make up your own style guide, tailoring it to your newsletter's unique needs. If your space is limited, for example, you may need to use more abbreviations than a newsletter that has plenty of space. Your own denomination probably has many special days, offerings, and programs that should be capitalized when they appear in your newsletter. The important thing is to establish a uniform style that suits your needs and to stick with it consistently from issue to issue.

The following easy-reference guide should answer some of your questions about how to capitalize and abbreviate the words and terms that appear most often in church newsletters. Use it as a start in compiling a style guide of your own. For additional guidance on capitalization, hyphenation, and spelling of specific words, look them up in the latest edition of *Webster's New Collegiate Dictionary*. For help on grammar and punctuation, see the latest edition of the *Chicago Manual of Style*.

I. Capitalization Guide
for Commonly Used Words and Terms

AD
Advent
agape (underlined or italicized)
all-church picnic
administrative board
AM
Anointed One (title of Jesus)
anthem
apostles, the apostle Paul, the great apostle; but: Apostle to the Gentiles
ascension
Ash Wednesday
B.A., M.A., Th.D. (and other academic degrees: periods after letters with no spaces between)
BC
benediction
Bible
Bible study
biblical
Boy Scouts
Bread of life (title of Jesus)
call to worship
centennial
children of Israel
Chosen People (the Hebrew people in the Bible)

Christmas
Church, the (when referring to the universal Church, past and present, or a specific local church; but: church board, church budget, church council, church conference)
church business administrator
Church School, Sunday School
Columbus Day
Commandments (referring to the Ten Commandments)
Communion
confirmands
confirmation
confirmation class
covered-dish dinner
Creator (referring to God)
Crucifixion Week; but: the crucifixion
Dead Sea Scrolls
deacons
Decalogue, the (referring to the Ten Commandments)
devil, the devil
director of Christian education
doxology
East, the; Middle East; Far East; the South (referring to a geographical section of the world or an individual nation)
east, eastern (direction)

Easter
Easter sunrise service
ekklesia (underlined or italicized)
elders
Epiphany
Eucharist
Evangelism Explosion (specific witness-training program)
evening worship
Exile (the captivity of the Jews in Babylon)
Exodus, the (escape of the Israelites from Egypt)
Father's Day
federal government
fellowship dinner
Flood, the (the universal Flood in the book of Genesis)
Garden of Eden
Gentile
God's Son (title of Jesus)
Golden Rule
Good Shepherd (title of Jesus)
gospel (the good news)
Gospel, the (of Matthew, Mark, Luke, or John)
gospel meeting, revival
Grandparents Day (national holiday)
Great Commission (Jesus' charge in Matt. 28:19-20)
Great Physician (title of Jesus)
Hanukkah
heaven
hell
High Priest (title of Jesus)
Holy Bible
Holy Communion
Holy Spirit
Holy Thursday
Holy Week
incarnation, the (of Christ)
Independence Day (national holiday)
invocation
King of kings (title of Jesus)
koinonia (underlined or italicized)
Labor Day
Lamb, Lamb of God (title of Jesus)
Last Supper, the (referring to this event in the life of Jesus)
Law (a section of the Bible)
Lay Witness Mission (specific faith-sharing program)
Lent
Lenten Season
Light of the world, the (title of Jesus)
living Bread, the (title of Jesus)
Lord of lords (title of Jesus)
Lord's Supper
Love Feast
Major Prophets (a section of the Bible)
Mass
Master, Master Teacher (title of Jesus)
Maundy Thursday
Memorial Day

Messiah (title of Jesus)
midweek prayer meeting
minister
minister of education
Minor Prophets (a section of the Bible)
Model Prayer (Lord's Prayer)
morning worship
Mother's Day
music minister
New Covenant
New Testament
New Year's Day
Old Covenant
Old Testament
outreach
Palm Sunday
Passion Week
Passover meal
Passover supper, the
pastor; but: Pastor John Jones
Pastoral Epistles (a section of the Bible)
Pauline Epistles (a section of the Bible)
Pentateuch (a section of the Bible)
Pentecost
PM
postlude
pot-luck dinner
prelude
processional
Promised Land (Canaan)
recessional
Redeemer (title of Jesus)
resurrection
revival, gospel meeting
sabbath, sabbath day
Saint Andrew, Saint Lawrence (and other saints of the Church: always capitalized)
Satan
Savior (title of Jesus)
scriptural
Scripture, Scriptures
Sea of Galilee
second coming of Christ
Son of man (title of Jesus)
Stations of the Cross
stewards
stewardship
Suffering Servant (title of Jesus)
Summer Church School
Sunday School, Church School
Synoptic Gospels (a section of the Bible)
Temple (the Temple in Jerusalem; otherwise, temple)
Ten Commandments
Thanksgiving Day (national holiday)
transfiguration, the
Trinity Sunday

triumphal entry
twelve, the (Jesus' disciples)
twelve apostles
twelve tribes of Israel
upper room
ushers
Vacation Bible School
Vacation Church School
Valentine's Day
Veteran's Day

visitation
West, the (a geographical section of the world or an individual nation)
west, western (direction)
Word of God (referring to the Bible)
work day
Yom Kippur
youth minister
Youth Week

II. Abbreviations for Books of the Bible

Old Testament

Gen.
Ex.
Lev.
Num.
Deut.
Josh.
Judg.
Ruth
1 Sam.
2 Sam.
1 Kin.
2 Kin.
1 Chr.
2 Chr.
Ezra
Neh.
Esther
Job
Ps.
Prov.
Eccl.
Song of Sol.
Isa.
Jer.
Lam.
Ezek.
Dan.
Hos.
Joel
Amos
Obad.
Jonah
Mic.
Nah.
Hab.
Zeph.
Hag.
Zech.
Mal.

New Testament

Matt.
Mark
Luke
John
Acts
Rom.
1 Cor.
2 Cor.
Gal.
Eph.
Phil.
Col.
1 Thess.
2 Thess.
1 Tim.
2 Tim.
Titus
Philem.
Heb.
Jas.
1 Pet.
2 Pet.
1 John
2 John
3 John
Jude
Rev.

List of Illustrations and Photographs

Index